MW01009175

Rapid Climate Change

Scott G. McNall

The book reviews the science of climate change and explains why it is one of the most difficult problems humanity has ever tackled. Climate change is a "wicked" problem bound up with problems of population growth, environmental degradation, and world problems of growing social and economic inequality. The book explores the politicization of the topic, the polarization of opinion, and the reasons why, for some, science has become just another ideology to be contested. How do humans assess risk? Why are they so bad at focusing on the future? How can we solve the problem of climate change? These are the questions this work answers.

Scott G. McNall is the Senior Advisor to the President for Sustainability at California State University, Chico. He was the founding Executive Director of the Institute for Sustainable Development at the university and served for three years in that capacity. He is Professor Emeritus of Sociology and has served as Provost for 13 years and Interim University President for almost one year.

Framing 21st Century Social Issues

The goal of this new, unique Series is to offer readable, teachable "thinking frames" on today's social problems and social issues by leading scholars. These are available for view on http://routledge.custom gateway.com/routledge-social-issues.html.

For instructors teaching a wide range of courses in the social sciences, the Routledge *Social Issues Collection* now offers the best of both worlds: originally written short texts that provide "overviews" to important social issues *as well as* teachable excerpts from larger works previously published by Routledge and other presses.

As an instructor, click to the website to view the library and decide how to build your custom anthology and which thinking frames to assign. Students can choose to receive the assigned materials in print and/or electronic formats at an affordable price.

Body Problems
Running and Living Long in a Fast-Food
Society
Ben Agger

Sex, Drugs, and Death
Addressing Youth Problems in American
Society
Tammy Anderson

The Stupidity Epidemic
Worrying About Students, Schools, and
America's Future
Joel Best

Empire Versus Democracy
The Triumph of Corporate and Military
Power
Carl Boggs

Contentious Identities
Ethnic, Religious, and Nationalist Conflicts
in Today's World
Daniel Chirot

The Future of Higher Education
Dan Clawson and Max Page

Waste and Consumption
Capitalism, the Environment, and the Life
of Things
Simonetta Falasca-Zamponi

Rapid Climate Change
Causes, Consequences, and Solutions
Scott G. McNall

The Problem of Emotions in Societies
Jonathan H. Turner

Outsourcing the Womb
Race, Class, and Gestational Surrogacy
in a Global Market
France Winddance Twine

Changing Times for Black Professionals
Adia Harvey Wingfield

Why Nations Go to War
A Sociology of Military Conflict
Mark Worrell

Rapid Climate Change
Causes, Consequences, and Solutions

Scott G. McNall
California State University, Chico

Routledge
Taylor & Francis Group

NEW YORK AND LONDON

First published 2011
by Routledge
270 Madison Avenue, New York, NY 10016

Simultaneously published in the UK
by Routledge
2 Park Square, Milton Park, Abingdon, Oxon OX14 4RN

Routledge is an imprint of the Taylor & Francis Group, an informa business

© 2011 Taylor & Francis

The right of Scott G. McNall to be identified as author of this work has been asserted by him in accordance with sections 77 and 78 of the Copyright, Designs and Patents Act 1988.

Typeset in Garamond and Gill Sans by EvS Communication Networx, Inc.

All rights reserved. No part of this book may be reprinted or reproduced or utilized in any form or by any electronic, mechanical, or other means, now known or hereafter invented, including photocopying and recording, or in any information storage or retrieval system, without permission in writing from the publishers.

Trademark Notice: Product or corporate names may be trademarks or registered trademarks, and are used only for identification and explanation without intent to infringe.

Library of Congress Cataloging in Publication Data
McNall, Scott G.
Rapid climate change : causes, consequences, and solutions / Scott G. McNall. — 1st ed.
p. cm. — (Framing 21st century social issues)
1. Social ecology. 2. Global environmental change. 3. Environmental policy. 4. Climatic changes—Forecasting. I. Title.
HM861.M36 2011
363.738'74—dc22
2010040161

ISBN13: 978-0-415-89203-2 (pbk)
ISBN13: 978-0-203-83424-4 (ebk)

Contents

Series Foreword

The world in the early 21st century is beset with problems—a troubled economy, global warming, oil spills, religious and national conflict, poverty, HIV, health problems associated with sedentary lifestyles. Virtually no nation is exempt, and everyone, even in affluent countries, feels the impact of these global issues.

Since its inception in the 19th century, sociology has been the academic discipline dedicated to analyzing social problems. It is still so today. Sociologists offer not only diagnoses; they glimpse solutions, which they then offer to policy makers and citizens who work for a better world. Sociology played a major role in the civil rights movement during the 1960s in helping us to understand racial inequalities and prejudice, and it can play a major role today as we grapple with old and new issues.

This series builds on the giants of sociology, such as Weber, Durkheim, Marx, Parsons, Mills. It uses their frames, and newer ones, to focus on particular issues of contemporary concern. These books are about the nuts and bolts of social problems, but they are equally about the frames through which we analyze these problems. It is clear by now that there is no single correct way to view the world, but only paradigms, models, which function as lenses through which we peer. For example, in analyzing oil spills and environmental pollution, we can use a frame that views such outcomes as unfortunate results of a reasonable effort to harvest fossil fuels. "Drill, baby, drill" sometimes involves certain costs as pipelines rupture and oil spews forth. Or we could analyze these environmental crises as inevitable outcomes of our effort to dominate nature in the interest of profit. The first frame would solve oil spills with better environmental protection measures and clean-ups, while the second frame would attempt to prevent them altogether, perhaps shifting away from the use of petroleum and natural gas and toward alternative energies that are "green."

These books introduce various frames such as these for viewing social problems. They also highlight debates between social scientists who frame problems differently. The books suggest solutions, both on the macro and micro levels. That is, they suggest what new policies might entail, and they also identify ways in which people, from the ground level, can work toward a better world, changing themselves and their lives and families and providing models of change for others.

Readers do not need an extensive background in academic sociology to benefit from these books. Each book is student-friendly in that we provide glossaries of terms for the uninitiated that are keyed to bolded terms in the text. Each chapter ends with questions for further thought and discussion. The level of each book is accessible to undergraduate students, even as these books offer sophisticated and innovative analyses.

Scott McNall, in his book on rapid climate change, addresses perhaps the profoundest problem of our age. As he and Al Gore indicate, we can solve all the other problems, but if we don't solve this one, our ice caps will melt and civilization will be imperilled. But McNall, a sociologist, goes beyond this ecological observation. He grounds climate change in population growth, the use and cost of energy, and abundant global economic inequalities. He ask why our climate is changing, what has caused this, and, most important, what we as individuals and larger groups can do to reverse this process. McNall straddles social science and natural science in his unique and highly readable treatment supported by ample scholarly evidence and argument.

Preface

Why write a book about climate change? Why write about something that doesn't seem to affect us? First, it *will* affect us and will strongly affect the lives of others and the lives of future generations. My own answer to these questions is part of the reason I wrote the book. I have spent some time over the last five years talking to friends and acquaintances about climate change. Often, when the discussion drifted around to climate change, sometimes at my instigation, sometimes at theirs, I would find people telling me that climate change was a hoax, or that it was not caused by humans, or that even if it was, it was not really a big problem. If there were a problem, we could solve it with technology, as we have solved so many other problems.

So this book is in part a response to all of those who have challenged me to be clearer, to explain again what the problem is, to explain how we can solve the problem, and to be optimistic. My students, in particular, have not wanted to listen to long lists of all the things that are wrong with the world; they want to know how they can create their own futures and what they can actually do about the problem of climate change.

There is another reason, too, for writing this book. Few Americans, to whom this book is primarily addressed, understand their impact on others. How many people know that we, who represent only 5 percent of the world's total population, use up 25 percent of the oil produced each year, or that we are responsible for producing 20 percent of all the world's greenhouse gases? How many of us really understand the limits of ecosystems or realize some resources are finite? Who understands that eventually there will be no more oil, lithium, bauxite, or potassium? We were raised to assume there were no limits and that our economy would continue to grow as though it were a perpetual motion machine.

I explain why climate change is regarded as one of the most difficult problems humanity has ever faced, and I take seriously the importance of understanding that climate change is simply part of a larger puzzle that must be solved. Climate change is the cause of ruined ecosystems and, if unchecked, will be responsible for food insecurity, water shortages, mass migrations, and political instability. But it is also caused by population growth, by global economic inequality, and by an economic system fueled by carbon. Climate change is not a problem that can be solved by throwing a switch on the wall. Solutions will require us to address population issues, economic inequality, and to devote resources to new technologies that can free us from a dependence on fossil fuels. It will require nations to do something they have seldom done before—act together to benefit future generations. We have something potentially more destructive than World War II in front of us. Can we rise to that challenge?

I first explore the science of climate change, and the reasons that are frequently offered by non-scientists to challenge the reality of what is happening to planet Earth. In Chapter II, I devote some energy to helping us understand why some believe that science is simply another ideology to be challenged, and why opinions on climate change have become polarized. Chapter III examines what we know about how human beings assess risk—and why we are so bad at taking into account what will happen in the future, and the major role emotions play in shaping our actions. In Chapter IV, I examine the new technologies that can help us solve the problem and identify actions the reader can take.

Daily events overtake all of us. We tend to focus on what is happening to us now, to our friends, and to our families. We have habits that we can't imagine changing. It is hard, but imperative, to remember that climate change is affecting us already and will shape our lives and those of our children, grandchildren, and the children of other nations. We must understand. From understanding comes action and change.

To
my grandchildren,
Eliot, Evan, and Madeline.

If future generations are to remember us with gratitude rather than contempt, we must leave them more than the miracles of technology. We must leave them a glimpse of what it was in the beginning, not just after we got through with it.

(Lyndon B. Johnson, 36th President of the United States, at the signing of the Wilderness Act, September 1964)

Our most basic common link is that we all inhabit this small planet. We all breathe the same air. We cherish our children's future. We are all mortal.

(John F. Kennedy, 35th President of the United States)

1: Why is the Earth Getting Warmer and What Difference Does it Make?

～～✕～～

Your great grandfather or great grandmother probably had a car. Each time they drove around, they added carbon dioxide (CO_2) to the air, and that CO_2 is still in the atmosphere. Why does that matter? It matters because, since the Industrial Revolution began, we have been pumping so much CO_2 into the atmosphere at increasing rates that the planet is now warming to dangerous levels with serious and irreversible consequences. The level of CO_2 is now higher than at any time in the last 650 thousand years. We are adding over eight billion tons of CO_2 to the atmosphere *every year* (Pearce 2007). Everything frozen on the planet is thawing. Yet the warming of the planet is not the only problem facing us. Other issues such as continued population growth, growing inequality, and destruction of the Earth's **ecosystems** must be addressed if we are to have a future. This chapter will explore the reasons for the warming of the Earth and the interrelationship between the problems that must be addressed. Your great grandparents did not know what the consequences of their actions would be. Today we know.

What is the Evidence that the Earth is Warming?

The Inuit who sees her village disappearing before her eyes, as the ice melts and breaks away, clearly understands that if her family is to have a future they need to move. In Yosemite National Park, one of the world's great treasures, we see trees dying because of a hotter and drier climate, as they become more susceptible to disease and pests. The chipmunks that tourists love to feed have migrated 400 feet further up, and the glaciers in the Sierra Nevada have shrunk by 50 percent. When I was a child living in Oregon, my parents took me to the Lava Beds National Monument and the Merrill Ice Caves. It was wonderful on a hot summer day to sit on the ice found in the caves. But in 1999 that ice started abruptly melting and is now entirely gone in most of the caves. This story, however, is nothing compared with the droughts that devastated grain harvests in Africa, leading to starvation, or the 35,000 people in Western

Europe, who died from a summer heat wave in 2003. There are many, many signs that our climate is changing. A few of them are:

- The Himalayan glaciers, which feed rivers in Pakistan, Afghanistan, India, and China, and provide 40 percent of the drinking water for half of the world's population, are receding.
- The hottest temperatures, since we first started recording them in the 1800s, have occurred in the last 25 years.
- Hurricanes, which are driven by warm, moist air from the Tropics, are becoming more frequent and intense.
- Western North America is drying out with the result that fires are more frequent in the summer and water for irrigation and household use becomes more expensive (Overpeck and Udall 2010).
- Spring now comes earlier and winter later in Europe and northern Asia, extending the growing season by up to three weeks.
- Buildings in Siberia and Alaska are sinking into the ground as the **permafrost** melts.
- Melting ice in the Arctic has reduced the time that polar bears can hunt, increasing the number of bear attacking humans, homes, and hunting camps as they move south looking for food.

How did it happen that the environmental systems of the Earth became so degraded that the planet is warming? The Earth is about 4.5 billion years old, and life forms (single-celled organisms) have been present for 3.8 billion years. Two hundred million years ago mammals made their first appearance. Sixty-five million years ago the dinosaurs died out. The genus *Homo* arrived on the scene about 2.5 million years ago. People who looked like us appeared 200,000 years ago and modern humans date from 25,000 years ago, when the Neanderthals died out as a separate species. Relatively speaking, then, we humans have been around for a very short time—less than 0.001 percent of Earth's history. For most of our existence we were hunters and gatherers with simple tools, and our impact on the planet was small. The early years of human existence were hard, dangerous, and cold, as we were still living in an ice age. Then, as the glaciers began to retreat, a new era, the **Holocene**, began 12,000 years ago. The melting glaciers caused sea levels to rise by 115 feet, and they are still rising as the warming continues. The impact of humans, who had lived on the planet a short time, was swift. Large mammals died out in the Holocene extinction, as they were hunted down by humans. Our numbers quickly grew: 100,000 years ago there were only one million of us, maybe even as few as 10,000 of us; in 1800 we numbered about 1.5 billion; now we number almost 6.8 billion; and by 2050, only 40 years from now, there will be over nine billion of us—nine billion people to feed, clothe, and shelter.

Planet Earth

As the Earth has been warming and continues to warm, we are living in the first geological epoch caused by humans, the **Anthropocene**. The Earth is a special place; it is the only planet in our solar system that supports human life. Looking back from deep space the Earth appears as a blue marble suspended in darkness. The richness of life on Earth is contrasted to the barren moonscape on the cover of this book. The Earth has evolved through many geological epochs with life forms changing along with each. We have evolved along with the Earth and are now living during a period uniquely suited to our success as a species. The Earth can be thought of as a stable, self-regulating system, of which we are a crucial part.

James Lovelock (2006), inventor, scientist, and author, has offered a useful metaphor for understanding how the Earth works. The **Gaia hypothesis**, named after the Greek goddess of the Earth, suggests that the living and non-living parts of the Earth form a complex interacting system that may be thought of as a single organism. The biosphere (the part of the Earth and its atmosphere in which living organisms exist) balances itself to support life. Lovelock developed this idea in the 1960s when he was working as a consultant for NASA on a project to determine whether life existed on Mars. What he noticed was that the atmosphere of Mars was in a state of chemical equilibrium with little oxygen, **methane**, or hydrogen, but with an abundance of carbon dioxide. Comparing the chemical mix of Earth's atmosphere to Mars, he reasoned, correctly, that there would be no life on Mars. He also reasoned that planets maintain a state of equilibrium and has suggested that they can be tipped out of one state into another. The Gaia hypothesis has interested many in the environmental community, but has received little support from the scientific community.

Nevertheless, the idea that we should think of the Earth as a closed system (see **systems theory**) that can be tipped out of balance is an important one. Up to this point, in Earth's 4.5-billion-year history, what has happened has had little to do with us. Now the evidence has mounted to the point where it is clear we have impacted Earth's biosphere. Tim Flannery (2009), a scientist, has extended the ideas of Lovelock. He notes that the Earth has what may be thought of as a "rind" composed of Earth's crust, air, and water, extending seven to eight miles below Earth's surface and 15 miles above it. It is this "rind" that sustains life. The Earth's crust is dynamic; as tectonic plates grind against one another they cause earthquakes, volcanic eruptions, and the movement of entire continents. Wind and rain erode rocks creating the mineral rich soil on which we grow our food. The photosynthesis of plants millions of years ago drew carbon out of the atmosphere and gives us the oil we pump from the ground today. The ocean is equally dynamic. Evaporation and precipitation recycle water from both the oceans and rivers. Rivers running into the sea pass over mineral-rich rocks and carry salt into the ocean. That salty water has its chemical structure changed by super-heated water from hydrothermal vents in mid-ocean with the result that the balance of salt stays the same. The recycling of water through evaporation and precipitation occurs every 40,000 years, and all of the water in the oceans passes through the hydrothermal vents every 10 to 100 million years. This has resulted in a remarkable state of stability in terms of the saltiness of the ocean. The smallest part of the rind is the atmosphere. Flannery (2009: 25) suggests a thought experiment. Imagine compressing the entire atmosphere and all of its gases about one thousand-fold until it became a liquid. At that point, it would be 500 times smaller than the ocean. The Earth's atmosphere is very thin. It is on this part of Earth's systems that we have had our greatest impact. Compared with two hundred years ago, the concentration of CO_2 in the atmosphere has increased by over 30 percent, and now stands at close to 390 ppm (parts per million). What does it mean to our lives and to the lives of future generations that CO_2 continues to build up in the atmosphere?

Global Warming

Earth's atmosphere is remarkably thin but like Goldilocks and the porridge, until recently, it was just right. Mars has virtually no atmosphere and is too cold for life and that of Venus is too thick and too hot. Without **greenhouse gases (GHGs)** surrounding our planet there would be no human life. What all greenhouse gases do is allow light from the Sun to penetrate the atmosphere and then trap a portion of the reflected radiation to warm lower portions of the atmosphere and heat the Earth. Over time the heat entering and leaving should balance out, leading to stable temperatures. We have known about this effect since it was first proposed by Joseph Fourier in 1824. We have also known about the potential for the Earth to warm beyond natural limits due to increasing concentrations of CO_2 since 1896, when Svante Arrhenius first advanced the idea. Naturally occurring greenhouse gases have kept our average world temperature around 59° Fahrenheit. However, global mean temperatures have been steadily increasing since the beginning of the Industrial Revolution. Though there have been fluctuations due to natural events such as volcanic eruptions (e.g. Mount Pinatubo in 1991) that temporarily lower temperature, because heat shielding sulfur is released into the atmosphere, the trend to higher temperatures has continued steadily upward. The average temperatures of the last five years appear to be the highest in thousands of years.

One of the most well-known studies of the rise of carbon dioxide in our atmosphere was conducted by Charles David Keeling, who started measuring concentrations in 1958 on the top of a mountain (Mauna Lea) on the big island of Hawaii. The reason for locating the observatory on a mountain top in the middle of the Pacific Ocean was that measurements of carbon dioxide would not be affected by industry. He started with the knowledge that before 1800 atmospheric concentrations were around 275 ppm and had been for several thousand years (scientists know this because they can measure the composition of the air trapped in polar ice over thousands of years). When he started his measurements in 1958 they were around 315 ppm and by the year 2000 they were 367 ppm. His findings were charted and they showed seasonal fluctuations from fall to spring and back but with a steady upward curve that came to be called the **Keeling Curve**. The reason for the variation from spring to fall is that in the spring plants and grasses turn green and draw in carbon dioxide, as part of the process of photosynthesis, and in the fall and winter the cycle reverses when the plants wilt and decay. One might think of the Earth breathing in and out on an annual basis (University of California, San Diego 2010). He was joined in his studies by one of his colleagues, Roger Revelle, who like Keeling was trying to understand how Earth's systems (the atmosphere, the oceans, the land) worked together. His focus was on the ocean, because the oceans absorb more CO_2 than anything else on the planet. What Revelle found was that the oceans were being increasingly taxed and were no longer absorbing CO_2 at the rate predicted by geoscientists. He reasoned that this could lead eventually to the warming of the planet (NASA 2010).

What does make up our atmosphere? There are 11 abundant greenhouse gases, of which nitrogen, oxygen, water vapor, carbon dioxide, methane, nitrous oxide, and ozone are the most important to the Earth's living organisms. In terms of volume, nitrogen (78 percent) and oxygen (21 percent) followed by argon (1 percent) make up the bulk of the dry atmosphere and have been stable for most of the Earth's recent history. They are called the **constant gases** for that very reason. Carbon dioxide is actually a tiny portion of the overall atmosphere (0.0383 percent). Nitrogen is an inert gas produced by volcanoes; it is removed from the air by nitrogen fixing bacteria and is an important part of the cycle of life. It stimulates plant growth. Oxygen is, of course, essential for life also and is exchanged between the atmosphere and life through the processes of photosynthesis and respiration. Plants take up carbon dioxide in the process of photosynthesis and release it as oxygen. It is also important for chemical breakdowns (oxidization) and for the degrading of minerals (weathering). We use argon, which is colorless and odorless, in the manufacture of light bulbs, insulated windows, and growing semiconductor crystals (Ritter 2009).

There are several **variable gases** including carbon dioxide, methane, ozone, and water vapor that make up our atmosphere. Water vapor is the most abundant of the variable gases with high concentrations near the Equator, over the oceans, and in the tropical rain forests; there is little to none at the Poles. Water vapor is not an important heat-trapping gas, because most of it stays in the atmosphere for short periods, three to seven days. There will be more, though, if there are warmer temperatures. Two of the variable gases will draw our concern—carbon dioxide and methane—because they have the greatest impact on our environment. As I noted, CO_2 makes up but a small amount of the atmosphere but it stays there for 100 to 500 years (Cook 2010), causing a cumulative build-up and gradual and inevitable warming. Because carbon dioxide is part of the process of photosynthesis huge quantities of carbon are stored or "locked"-up plant matter: coal, oil, peat, and natural gas. When we burn fossil fuels, pave grasslands for housing developments, or cut down trees to create pastures or plant crops, CO_2 is released and builds up in the atmosphere. The volume of carbon dioxide in the atmosphere has increased 30 percent in the last 300 years; the highest it has been for 650,000 years (Intergovernmental Panel on Climate Change 2007). CO_2 now accounts for 80 percent of all greenhouse gas emissions. Carbon dioxide causes **radiative forcing** and changes the balance between solar radiation entering and leaving the Earth's atmosphere. You could think of it as a gas that thickens the atmosphere.

Methane concentrations mirror those of CO_2 and are now 148 percent higher than during pre-industrial times. We add about 350–500 million tons of methane to the air by raising livestock, mining coal, drilling for oil, cultivating rice, and piling up garbage in landfills. Methane is a dangerous greenhouse gas, because it is *25 times more potent as a heat-trapping gas than CO_2* over a 100-year time horizon, but 72 times more potent over a 20-year period. Billions of tons of methane and carbon are embedded in the oceans and in frozen peat. If the permafrost melts, it could tip the Earth out of the long period of stable climate we have enjoyed.

Aerosols also make up part of our atmosphere and they, too, impact the climate. Aerosols, which are created when we burn fossil fuels or **biomass** (forests, for example), absorb and emit heat, reflect light, and, depending on their properties, either cool or warm the atmosphere. They are important to mention, because we will discuss them again in Chapter IV, when we focus on solutions. *Sulfate aerosols* (which were responsible for acid rain and are the result of burning coal or volcanic activity) have a cooling effect, because they bounce solar radiation back into space. *Black carbon*, or soot, has a warming or cooling effect depending on whether it stays in the atmosphere or is deposited on the ground. Soot deposited on glaciers and snow fields speeds the process of melting, because it changes the **albedo effect**, which refers to the fact that solar radiation bounces off of white surfaces and is reflected back into space. When it stays suspended in the air, it masks the actual warming that all soot causes. In rural India, where brown clouds and pollution cloud the sky, it masks up to 50 percent of surface warming. Soot has declined in the United States and northern European countries but its impact is pronounced in the Tropics and in Asia (Environmental Protection Agency 2009) We continue to alter our atmosphere. When will we start to feel the greatest impacts?

Tipping Points

Some fear we have reached the point at which the burning of fossil fuels and the transformation of the land will force the Earth out of the pattern of regular freezes and thaws that has lasted for more than a million years. (We will say more about the regularity of Earth's cycles below.) Seven **tipping points** (or elements as they are called by climate scientists) have been identified, any one of which would produce an epic disaster (Lenton, et al. 2009), because each tipping point is part of a larger system. A change in one system does not allow us to predict precisely what will happen in another system. The effect could be more or it could be less. But at some point, these changes add up to a change of the entire system. For example, as **climate change** warms and melts glaciers, it reduces the albedo effect, which in turn speeds up warming and causes more melting. Melting glaciers will eventually lead to rising seas, which will cause the loss of productive farm land for millions, which will cause populations to move to less productive areas, leading to loss of grasslands and forest cover, which will speed the process of warming.

1. **The permafrost.** Fred Pearce (2007: 77–79) has described the permafrost as a doomsday machine, a ticking bomb ready to explode at some unknown time in the future. The western Siberian peat bog is about 400,000 square miles, equivalent to the size of France and Germany combined. It formed over thousands of years as plant matter slowly decomposed, locking up about one-fourth of all the carbon sequestered on Earth since the last ice age. As this frozen mass begins to thaw, it is releasing, by one estimate, methane at a rate of 100,000 tons a day, which is equivalent to the total of all the man-made greenhouse gases released by the United States in a year. Methane is also bubbling up from the sea floor where it is trapped in deep-sea sediments called methane hydrates. As ocean temperatures rise, the fear is that these might be released in a giant "belch" as happened before in Earth's history, before humans were around to witness the effects (Archer, Buffet, and Brovkin 2009).

2. **Monsoons.** Leverman and his colleagues (2009) have noted that the Indian **monsoon** is essential for the livelihoods of several hundred million people, as it generates the necessary water for much of the agriculture in the subcontinent—India, Bangladesh, Nepal, and Pakistan. Ninety percent of India's water depends on the monsoons. Almost half of the world's population could be affected as climate change causes a delay in the start of the monsoon season, less summer rain, and longer delays between periods of rain (Diffenbaugh, et al. 2009).

3. **Bodele Depression in Chad.** Winds blowing off the **Bodele Depression**, an area of almost 10,000 square miles on the Saharan plain, carry 700,000 tons of sedimentary material into the air. Some of this dust ends up on the South American continent, helping to bring nutrients to the Amazonian rainforest. It blocks sunlight in some areas, lowering temperatures, causing rain in others. It influences land and marine ecosystems, although not all effects are well understood. The concern of researchers (Washington, et al. 2009) is that anthropogenic (human-caused) actions could cause these winds to change in as little as one season, because at one point in the last 10,000 years these winds did stop blowing.

4. **Amazonian rainforest.** The Amazonian rainforest is one of the world's great carbon sinks, but the Amazon is turning brown (Mahli, et al. 2009). In the last 40 years, 20 percent of the forest has been cut down, more than in the previous 450 years since European colonization. The forests are disappearing as loggers, some legal, many not, have moved in to cut mahogany and other prized hardwoods for international trade. The roads they create to haul out the logs become super highways for squatters, speculators and ranchers looking for land. Our hunger for meat has caused land to be cleared for ranches. Trees are bulldozed and burned to clear fields to plant soybeans and other crops that make their way to world markets to feed farm-raised salmon, chicken, and us.

5. **The oceans.** We have destroyed entire fisheries by our appetite for cod, bluefin tuna, rockfish, sardines and other species; we have pushed the population of different whales nearly to the point of extinction; our garbage has created a swirling mass of plastic, the size of the state of Texas, in the Pacific Ocean. Plastic is broken down by the waves and sunlight into small particles that enter the entire food chain. We are also changing the chemical balance of the ocean. The oceans, which cover 71 percent of Earth's surface, are important to life and to planetary stability. Along with plants, the oceans absorb about 50 percent of all the CO_2 emitted each year. As atmospheric CO_2 is absorbed by the ocean, it forms carbonic acid, which can affect the growth of shellfish such as crabs, lobsters, mussels, and clams. Recent studies have shown the oceans are becoming increasingly acidic, and at rates ten times higher than had been predicted by earlier climate models (Wooten, Pfister, and Forester 2008). A sobering new report indicates that the oceans face a fundamental and irreversible ecological transformation not seen in millions of years (Hoegh-Guldberg and Bruno 2010).

6. **The ocean conveyor belt.** The oceans serve to balance heat across the globe, as well as balance the amount of greenhouse gases. The circulation of water from warmer to colder regions is referred to as the **theromohaline circulation** and it is caused by heat (therm) and salinity (haline). In a journey that takes 1,000 years to complete, warm water moves from the far Pacific, through the Tropics, up the coast of Africa, back down and around until it hits the cold and salty water from the North Atlantic, plunges to the ocean floor at a rate of almost five billion gallons a second, and forms a cold current flowing southward down the coast of South America and back out into the Pacific where it starts over. Ten thousand years ago this conveyor belt stopped, creating an ice age that lasted for 1,000 years. The current stopped because, as the glaciers melted in North America, they created a giant pool of water over what are now the Great Lakes, which was held in place by a giant ice dam to the east. When the dam broke, billions of gallons of fresh water poured into the Atlantic Ocean, changing its salinity and disrupting the **ocean conveyor belt**. The change was swift. Recent research has suggested that the Younger Dryas, or mini-Ice Age, took hold in just ten years (Ravilious

2009). The melting of the Greenland ice sheets and the flooding of the Atlantic with fresh water could bring on a new ice age. Though this idea has received a lot of attention (see Chapter II), most climate scientists do not believe such an abrupt change is likely (Hoffmann and Rahmstorf 2009).

7. **Polar sea ice.** A research team (Ballantyne, et al. 2010) working on Ellesmere Island in the Canadian Arctic have found evidence from a period known as the Pliocene Epoch, dating from 2.6 to 5.3 million years ago, that the Arctic was once much warmer, as we knew. There were fish, bears, frogs, three-toed horses, badgers, and other animals. The importance of the team's finding was to demonstrate that this condition existed when the concentration of CO_2 levels in the atmosphere stood at 400 ppm, a limit we are now approaching. The Arctic sea ice is declining at a rate of 11 percent a decade, which means you will probably all live to see ice-free Arctic summers. In the Antarctic, glaciers continue to fall into the ocean. One the size of the state of Connecticut broke off of the Ross Ice Shelf in 2000. If all the ice in Antarctic melted (which it is not likely to do), ocean levels would rise, everywhere, by 200 feet.

Scientific Consensus

There is, among climate scientists, enormous consensus about our changing planet. With each new report on the oceans, the atmosphere, ice shelves, the length of growing seasons, and the migration of mammals, the certainty that human activity is causing climate change increases. So, too, does the fear of the possibility that, if we do not act soon to reverse the build-up of CO_2 in the atmosphere, it will be too late. Sometimes it seems as though scientists might not be in agreement about climate change, because they offer different, though not contradictory, ideas about what will happen when. No climate model can tell us precisely when the Earth will warm by 3° or 4° Fahrenheit. We know for sure that CO_2 build-up causes the Earth to warm and we know for sure that as the planet warms it will speed up processes that reinforce one another. The predictions vary because scientists sometimes use different models to describe and account for what is happening. Virtually all models are a combination of what we know about the circulation of the oceans (salt content and heat); about the transfer of heat and moisture from the land and vegetation to the atmosphere; and about the movement of air, temperature, and the formation of clouds. Cloud formation is particularly difficult to account for in the models, as is what will happen as methane releases from permafrost and the ocean sea bed. But these models are becoming increasingly accurate, as more and more data are collected. They are tested based on both their ability to portray accurately what has happened in the past, as well as what will happen in the future. If anything, the models have been conservative, for the Arctic sea ice has melted much more rapidly than predicted by the Intergovernmental Panel on Climate Change (IPCC) models.

As we will see in the next chapter, many have sought to discredit the predictions of climate scientists and/or simply to deny that change could be attributed to human action. Their reasons for doing so are grounded in culture, politics, and a lack of understanding about basic science. Let us quickly examine some of the reasons offered by those who deny humans are the cause of global warming.

- **Natural cycles**. "The Earth is simply going through a natural cycle and has been warming since the last Ice Age." It is true that the Earth goes through natural cycles, which affect climate. They are referred to as the **Milankovitch cycles**, named after the Serbian engineer who calculated them while imprisoned during World War I. The three cycles, and the frequency of their occurrence, are as follows. *Eccentricity* refers to the shape of Earth's orbit around the Sun, which varies from a circle to an ellipse every 100,000 years, and affects the length of the seasons in the northern and southern hemispheres; *precession*, or the wobbling of the Earth on its axis, which occurs every 21–23,000 years; and *tilt*, relative to the plane of the Earth, which occurs every 41,000 years. It is the tilt of the axis, from 21.5° to 24.5° that drives the ice ages. We are now in the middle of tilt. Our current climate, then, cannot be explained in terms of natural cycles.
- **Sunspots and solar flares**. "It's sunspots." Solar flares have been measured for a short period of time, but the findings are clear. Solar radiation pulses occur every 11 years and account only for very small variations in temperature, perhaps 0.2° C. (See the website for the National Oceanic and Atmospheric Administration [NOAA] for a list of frequently asked questions about climate change.)
- **What about the weather**? "It's colder, not warmer." Our local newspaper often carries letters to the editor offering evidence that global warming must be a hoax because it was cold on the writer's vacation in Florida; because New England had a lot of snow; because Afghanistan had some of the coldest winters ever recorded at the beginning of the 21st century; and/or because the high Sierras are finally covered with snow and they can go skiing. All of these things are true, but have nothing to do with rapid climate change. Climate is, *by definition*, about events that take place over decades, centuries, and millennia. The weather is something we *personally experience* every day and our response is culturally determined. That is, we have cultural definitions of what it means to be comfortable. We expect to be cool in the summer when it is hot, and warm in the winter when it is cold and achieve this with cooling and heating systems. And it is the weather that gets reported on the evening news, not climate change. It is also the case that many reporters take extreme weather events to "prove" that the climate is changing or that it is not, which creates confusion and suspicion about the findings of climate scientists (see Chapter II). The reality is that extreme weather events, such as

Hurricane Katrina in 2005, and the deadly heatwave in Europe in 2003, are part of a larger pattern of climate change.

We have examined briefly the science behind global warming, and noted that the planet is warming because of human actions. Scientist after scientist has sounded the alarm bell and been dumbfounded that we cannot get people to see the consequences of their actions. The causes, as well as the effects of climate change, are part of an intricate web of social, political, and social behaviors with serious consequences. How might we understand the interplay between these factors?

Thinking about the Systems that Affect our Lives

In 1972, a group of politicians, businessmen, and scientists called the *Club of Rome* commissioned a study that modeled the relationship between five variables: population, industrialization, pollution, food production, and resource depletion. The model was based in system dynamics (see systems theory), which studies how the parts of complex systems relate to one another and how change in one variable drives changes to the entire system. The book that grew out of the Club of Rome's efforts by Donella Meadows and her colleagues (1972), *The Limits to Growth*, was seen by some as reflecting the concerns first raised by Thomas Malthus in his *An Essay on the Principle of Population* (1798). Malthus had assumed that population growth would eventually outrun the available food supply. What the authors demonstrated was that there were limits to growth, whether it was population, the food supply, or a growing economy.

If we followed a business-as-usual model, eventually living standards would stagnate, as more and more human capital and resources were diverted to mitigate the consequences of growth, for example, pollution, soil degradation, and declining natural resources such as coal, oil, manganese, or any other resource that was finite. Their goal was to find a model in which Earth's systems and human needs would be in balance. Meadows and her colleagues were among the first to use the concept of **overshoot**, an unsustainable state. There were hard *planetary limits* to the "rate at which humanity can extract resources (crops, grass, wood, fish) and emit wastes (greenhouse gases, toxic substances) without exceeding the productive or absorptive capacities of the world." There are three stages of overshoot and they are always the same:

- A period of growth, acceleration, and rapid change.
- A second stage in which one hits a limit or barrier, beyond which the system may not safely go.
- A delay or mistake in the perceptions and the responses that try to keep the system within bounds.

- The model is one driven by exponential growth in population, industrial production, and rising levels of consumption, which run up against finite limits in terms of land, water, and clean air.

If this sounds like our world today, it is. The book was updated in 2004, *Limits to Growth: The 30-Year Update*, and its conclusions about finite limits are proving true. As the authors point out, global grain production peaked in 1984 as did marine catches in 1988; both have been on a steep decline since then. There were global food riots in 2008, as the prices of wheat, corn, and rice sharply escalated (Karlin 2010). We have, in short, picked the low-hanging fruit, pumped the oil which was easily accessible, dammed the rivers we could, mined the coal, tin, bauxite, and iron ore that was readily available. Criticisms of the model have focused on the fact that it does not account for technological fixes or human creativity. That is, we *might* find new sources of energy and we *might* be able to limit our impact on Earth's ecosystems, and free-market mechanisms *might* be able to develop solutions, but all depend on the ability of people to make the right choices about something that will happen in the future. So far, as we will show in Chapter III, "Calculating the Odds: How We Think about Risk and Climate Change," we have seldom focused on making such choices.

Meadows and her colleagues are not the only ones who have pondered how complex societies unravel. Tainter (1988: 195) examined over 20 cases of societies that collapsed, from ancient regimes to ones in the present. Large, complex organizations require continued investments just to maintain the status quo. "This investment comes in such forms as increasing size of bureaucracies, increasing specialization of bureaucracies, cumulative organizational solutions, increasing costs of legitimizing activities, and increasing costs of internal control and external defense." The least costly solutions are quickly exhausted and with each new organizational problem that arises solutions "must be developed … at increasing cost and declining marginal returns" (Tainter 1988: 195). Societies collapse as they invest more and more heavily in strategies that yield proportionately less.

Jared Diamond (2005), in *Collapse: How Societies Choose to Fail or Succeed*, focuses on the environmental reasons for the collapse of societies. He identifies such factors as over-fishing and hunting, overpopulation, deforestation and habitat destruction, and soil erosion as some of the factors that contributed to the collapse of past societies. He also lists some new reasons why societies might collapse in the future, such as human-induced climate change, energy shortages, and the build-up of toxins in our environment. However, he sees population, or too many people for existing resources, as a primary reason, along with the culture of a society. It is our culture and our values that shape our relationship to the natural world that determine whether or not we make wise choices for future generations. As the famous historian Arnold Toynbee (*The Study of History*, 1934–61) suggested, "civilizations die from suicide, not by murder." How can we make wise choices?

Sustainability

The First World Climate conference was held in 1979, and shortly after that the United Nations formed the World Commission on Environment and Development, chaired by Gro Harlem Brundtland. The Brundtland Commission, as it came to be known, was created to address growing concerns "about the accelerating deterioration of the human environment and natural resources and the consequences of that deterioration for economic and social development" (United Nations 1983). The Commission issued its report in 1987, *Our Common Future*, and defined **sustainability**: "Sustainable development is development that meets the needs of the present without compromising the ability of future generations to meet their own needs" (Brundtland 1987).

The report underscored the fact that we must meet the needs of the world's poor today, as well as tomorrow, and it stressed that our current impact on the environment was a challenge to the needs of future generations. Poverty was the *result*, not the *cause*, of environmental degradation. Thus, a sustainable future is one in which economic, social, and environmental needs would be balanced. The path to sustainability is a difficult one. Why? One obvious reason is that some resources on our planet are finite and we will simply run out of them.

Peak Everything

M. King Hubbert was a geophysicist who, when he worked for Shell Oil Company, predicted in 1956 that the amount of oil in the world was finite. He anticipated, correctly, that oil production in the continental United States would peak in the early 1970s and decline from that point forward. He did not anticipate nor take into his calculations the possibility that we would be drilling for oil thousands of feet below the ocean's floor. He did note, though, that once extraction became more and more difficult, it would be reflected in the increased price of the commodity. It is costly and messy to drill for oil in oceans and it is environmentally costly to extract oil from tar sands or oil shale, all of which is reflected in the price. **Hubbert peak theory** has been applied to natural gas, coal, uranium, copper, and precious metals such as lithium now needed for batteries to power electric cars, computers, and cell phones. Hubbert (1976), who was a great believer in the possibilities of technology, wondered about how we might adapt to a post-peak world.

> Our principal constraints are cultural. During the last two centuries we have known nothing but exponential growth and in parallel we have evolved what amounts to an exponential-growth culture, a culture so heavily dependent upon the continuance of exponential growth for its stability that it is incapable of reckoning with problems of non-growth.
>
> (Hubbert 1976)

Following on Hubbert's work, Richard Heinberg (2007: 4), who has written extensively about peak oil, noted that we are reaching a peak for a lot more than just oil. By the end of the century we will see a decline in all of the following:

- Population.
- Grain production.
- Uranium production for nuclear power plants.
- Climate stability.
- Fresh water per capita.
- Arable land in agricultural production.
- Wild fish harvests.
- Extractable metals and minerals.

How soon these related declines will occur is a matter of debate. But we know we are entering an age of limits and of uncertainty.

Global Trends

The U.S. National Intelligence Council (2008) issued a report noting what we could anticipate by the year 2025. In terms of climate change, they identified two potential winners: Russia and Canada. Canada is a winner in the global climate war, because it will be spared intense hurricanes and intense heat and "climate change could open up millions of square miles to development." As Canada warms, growing seasons can be extended, and as ice melts from the Arctic opening up sea lanes year around, Canada can become a major geopolitical power. If you don't want to move to Canada, consider the opportunities the National Security Council sees for Russia:

> Russia has the most to gain from increasingly temperate weather. Russia has vast untapped reserves of natural gas and oil in Siberia and offshore in the Arctic, and warmer temperatures should make the reserves considerably more accessible. This would be a huge boon to the Russian economy, as presently 80 percent of the country's exports, and 32 percent of government revenues derive from the production of energy and raw materials.
>
> (National Intelligence Council 2008: 52)

It is a certainty, say national security analysts, that by 2050 we will see increased pressures for energy, food, and water. Demands for coal, gas, and oil will continue with the reality that new "green" energy sources (see Chapter IV) can only make up a small fraction of growing demands.

Global Inequalities

Climate change is unlike other problems. It is because we now understand that we live in a world of interdependence, in which we share one planet. It is also unlike other problems because *the effects of climate change are unevenly distributed, falling most heavily on the world's poor and on future generations.* Our ability to cope with climate change is unequal. "In rich countries, coping with climate change to date has largely been a matter of adjusting thermostats … By contrast, in the Horn of Africa it means that crops fail and people go hungry" (Watkins 2007/08: 9). *The richest countries in the world* (the United States, Canada, the United Kingdom, Germany, France), with only 15 percent of the world's population, *generate half of all the world's CO_2 emissions.* The average U.S. citizen generates five times the amount of carbon (21 tons) as the average Chinese citizen (3.8 tons). Yes, China is now leading the world in terms of total carbon emissions but they do so with a population of 1.3 billion, almost a billion people more than the United States. If *carbon budgets* were allocated evenly across the world's developed countries on the basis of population, and limited so that the world had a chance to keep temperatures from increasing beyond 3.6° Fahrenheit (which it will do because of warming already in the pipeline), the United States would be "bankrupt" in only six years; China would take 24, and the European Union would run out in 12 years (Giles 2009). There is growing concern, of course, that the entire planet could be bankrupt as countries such as India and China continue to improve the lives of their citizens, by doing what we have done—consuming non-renewal resources.

The burdens of global warming do not and will not fall evenly on the citizens of the world. Desmond Tutu, former Archbishop of Cape Town and winner of the Nobel Peace Prize, posed a set of questions.

> How does an impoverished woman in Malawi adapt when more frequent droughts and less rainfall cut production? Perhaps by cutting already inadequate household nutrition, or by taking her children out of school. How does a slum dweller living beneath plastic sheets and corrugated tin in a slum in Manila or Port-au-Prince adapt to the threat posed by more intense cyclones? And how are people living in the great deltas of the Ganges and Mekong supposed to adapt to the inundation of homes and lands?
>
> (Tutu 2007/08: 26)

The poor of the world are seldom in a position to adapt to climate shocks or environmental disasters. Consider what it would be like to live on $2.50 a day. Half (3.34 billion) of the entire world's population does so (World Bank 2010). Could you? It is important to remember such facts as the following, when considering how to balance human social and economic needs with environmental needs.

- We are adding 75 million people to the planet each year and each new person will have to be supported by increasingly scarcer and lower-quality resources (Erlich and Erlich 2009: 36).
- The most rapid population growth is in the world's poorest countries. India's population will reach 1.45 billion people by 2025, and countries in sub-Saharan Africa will add 350 million in the same period.
- There are 2.2 billion children in the world; half of them, 1.1 billion, live in poverty with limited access to adequate shelter, water, or health services.
- About 27–28 percent of all children in developing countries are estimated to be underweight or stunted.
- The world's wealthiest countries, or 20 percent (29 out of 195), account for about 75 percent of all consumption; the middle consume around 22 percent; and the poor make up the remainder—which is 3 percent of all consumption (Global Issues 2010).

Water Insecurity

Water is a special problem because we cannot live without it. Only 1–2 percent of the world's water is drinkable. More people die every year from water-borne diseases than die of hunger or war. Over 1 billion people have inadequate access to drinking water and 2.6 billion lack basic sanitation (Watkins 2006). Close to two million children die every year from diarrhea. Most of the world's fresh water is in North America and we use a lot of it. In the United States one of us uses an average of 160 gallons a day, most of which goes to flush toilets and water lawns and shrubs. In developing countries millions of women walk miles a day to get water for drinking and cooking. For those families who do not have indoor plumbing, the average consumption is 5.4 gallons of water a day. Consider trying to get through the day on only 5.4 gallons of water.

Lack of access to water and inadequate sanitation are primary drivers of poverty and inequality. "They claim millions of lives, destroy livelihoods, compromise dignity and diminish prospects for economic growth. Poor people, especially women and children, bear the brunt of the human costs" (Watkins 2006: ii). Many of the poor of the world depend on rainfall to water their crops and if the rains do not come, there is little hope of a decent life. As urban populations continue to grow, demand for water in the cities shifts what little water is available to the small farmer away to urban dwellers, deepening poverty in rural areas. But not all urban dwellers have access to clean water, because the poor often depend on infrastructure that is degrading. It is one reason that Mexicans drink more bottled water than the citizens of any other country, 62 gallons per person per year. That's twice as much as we consume in the United States. The developing countries (India, China, and Indonesia) have all attracted the focus of the companies selling bottled water, and their selling point is simple: Our water is safe! The result is plastic bottles littering the countryside (Johnson 2010). Water may be the new oil.

Finally, even the land that is available to the poor of the African continent is being removed from their control. Wealthy oil-rich countries such as Saudi Arabia and the Arab Emirates, as well as China, have been buying up millions of acres, along with the water, in order to provide food for their own countries. Lack of land and water can lead to genocide, epidemics, failed states, and civil war (Solomon 2010). Forests are cut down to feed growing populations, as fossil aquifers are pumped down to feed the demands of consumers, and animals are hunted down in the rainforest of the Congo to feed a demand for meat in the cities.

Failed States

Failed states are ones that cannot provide basic services for their citizens, such as water, sanitation, and education. They are characterized by deep social divisions and refugees fleeing civil wars to safer countries. The top ten failed states in the world are, in order, Somalia, Chad, Sudan, Zimbabwe, the Democratic Republic of the Congo, Afghanistan, Iraq, the Central African Republic, Guinea, and Pakistan (*Foreign Policy* 2010). These are also states that are experiencing rapid population growth and environmental degradation. If you live in the Congo, you would have a 50–50 chance of being under the age of 14, where population growth continues at 3 percent a year in spite of a civil war, high infant mortality, and water-borne diseases (*Foreign Policy* 2010). Afghanistan and Pakistan will both, as we noted above, soon be faced with less water.

The Challenges we Face

The challenges facing the world as a whole are the interrelated problems of population growth, climate change, global inequality, and the degradation of Earth's ecosystems (Brown 2009: 9). As we will learn in Chapter IV ("What is the Future Worth?"), we cannot solve the problems in isolation. Earlier in the chapter, we presented models that demonstrated continued exponential growth was not possible. Yet our economic system has been grounded under the assumption that growth can and must continue apace. It is estimated that from 60–70 percent of the entire United States economy is based on consumption. Any downturn in consumption, as has happened with the recent economic reversal in the world economy, can produce rapid changes in people's overall economic welfare as jobs are lost, mortgage payments missed, and plans deferred. Population continues to be a driver putting pressure on existing resources. Billions of people in the world go to bed hungry at night, and have increasingly limited access to land and water. They would like the same kind of lives that the majority of those who live in Europe and North America have. We need to figure out how we, as *global citizens*, can live sustainable lives and allow others to do so also. This will not be easy.

For example: *the Gulf oil spill* that began on April 20, 2010, and continued through the spring and summer, caused almost 200 million of gallons of oil to flow into the Gulf of Mexico. The costs of the spill, which occurred when the drilling rig leased by British Petroleum (BP) blew up, will total billions of dollars. The oil caused the shutdown of fishing in the Gulf, polluted wetlands, destroyed ecosystems, coated sea birds with oil, and caused the stock of BP to plummet. It was the greatest environmental disaster in U.S. history and it occurred because we were drilling, in deep ocean waters for oil. Some called for a moratorium on drilling, pointing to the devastating environmental loses. The governor of Florida called for a ban on drilling off the coasts of Florida, whose multi-billion-dollar-a-year tourist industry depends on white sands and ocean breezes unpolluted by the stench of oil.

However, many in Louisiana, the state hardest hit in terms of the destruction of ecosystems, called for drilling to restart. Why? There are 35,000 jobs connected with the drilling and almost 30 percent of the U.S. domestic supply of oil comes from the Gulf. Shutting down drilling would cause a spike in prices at the pump and a loss of jobs. But other people lost jobs: those who depended on fishing for shrimp, harvesting oysters or crabs, or taking people on chartered fishing trips. Some of these workers were hired temporarily by BP to help with the clean-up, but for many their lives will be changed forever as they depended on a healthy ecosystem to earn their living. No one knows, at this point, how long it will take for the ecosystems to recover.

Causes and Effects

In this one incident, we can see the difficulties of balancing social, economic, and environmental interests, but it is a challenge to which we must rise. Climate change is a serious problem and something we must deal with because, if we do not, the social, economic, and environmental systems on which we *all* depend could collapse. These systems are tightly interwoven. *Causes* and *effects* are mutually reinforcing. Free-market capitalism focused on exponential growth is a cause. This growth has been powered by fossil fuels, which are at the root of the problem. So, too, are population growth, over-fishing, and destruction of ocean ecosystems, worldwide consumption habits, deforestation, land transformation, and poverty. Poverty causes people to focus on the immediate needs of their families, which in turn can lead to the destruction of rainforests and the decimation of endangered species, such as the great apes.

Such *causes* result in *effects* such as desertification, increased poverty, water shortages, which lead to political conflict, failed states, and people migrating across borders seeking resources that have finite limits. *Climate change is a reality driven by human behavior*. How do we solve problems of energy, population growth, and climate change? Some have suggested that these problems will be solved the same way other problems have been solved in human history—through technology and human ingenuity. The possibility of technology being the answer to this set of interrelated problems will be explored in the final chapter. But some people continue to believe there is no problem to solve. As we will see in the next chapter, the very idea of climate change and climate science is challenged as "junk" by some. The topic of climate change has become highly politicized. Part of the reason it has become politicized is that some see the very notion of limits as a challenge to their way of life.

DISCUSSION QUESTIONS

1. What is the scientific evidence that the climate of the Earth is changing? Is there scientific consensus about climate change? Is there any evidence to suggest that climate change is not caused by humans?
2. Why have some argued that the problem of climate change is the greatest challenge ever facing humanity?
3. What actually causes climate change and what are the immediate as well as the anticipated effects of climate change?
4. Why is a systems approach essential for understanding climate change and for solving the problems associated with it? What are the problems that must be addressed if the problem of climate change is to be solved?
5. Historically, what has caused societies to collapse? Are these same factors operating today?

II: The Cassandra Problem

꘍

Cassandra was a Greek mythological character, to whom Apollo gave prophetic powers in order to win her love. Cassandra spurned him but rather than take back his gift, he took revenge by decreeing that her prophecies were never to be believed. Many of those who write about rapid climate change, the degradation of the environment, and the fact that the Earth may tip into a dangerous state of disequilibrium, are often treated like modern-day Cassandras. This chapter explores the reasons why some people do not believe in climate change, how the media shapes our views, and how and why some individuals and organizations have worked to sow seeds of doubt.

Shaping Public Opinion

Why do people believe the things they do? Where do they get their information about our changing planet? What are some of the factors that account for shifts in public opinion? And, why do Americans, in particular, fail to face up to the evidence?

Going to the Movies

The 2004 film, *The Day After Tomorrow*, grossed over $500 million worldwide, and sold an estimated 30 million tickets in the United States. The movie's hero, Jack Hall, survives the collapse of an ice shelf in the Antarctic and returns to warn his fellow countrymen about abrupt and cataclysmic changes that will occur because of global warming. He tells the Vice President of the United States about his fears, but he is ignored. Then, extreme weather events take place throughout the world—huge balls of hail rain down on Tokyo, tornadoes destroy Los Angeles, and a tidal wave washes over Manhattan. Jack briefs the President and people are advised to move south of an east–west line drawn across the country, because three massive super cells will pull freezing air to the ground creating a new ice age. People move, and as Jack predicts, Antarctic conditions prevail in the north. Jack's son, who has survived the tidal wave that washed over Manhattan, is holed up with his friends and burning books in the New York Public Library to keep warm. Jack begins his trek across a frozen wasteland to rescue him.

The movie unleashed a storm of controversy; some came from critics focused on the hyperbole and used the movie to claim that "junk" science was fueling debates about climate change. Scientists formed panels and took the opportunity to make the point that humans were causing the planet to warm but that climate change would never occur as quickly as portrayed in the movie. But did the movie actually change people's attitudes? Anthony Leiserowitz (2004), whose research focuses on how we perceive risk, found that watching the movie had a considerable impact. Watchers were more likely to say they would purchase a fuel-efficient car, talk to others about climate change, give money or join groups to take action, and more likely to vote for a Democratic candidate in the 2004 Presidential election. Did this cause an overall shift in public opinion? No, because only 10 percent of adults (those 18 and over) in the United States saw the movie; so while it was controversial and changed the minds of those who watched it, it did not cause a shift in public opinion. It did not in part because the general message of the movie—humans are the cause of climate change— was not reinforced in other media and because the messages from the media about climate change are mixed.

Reporting the News

Felicity Barringer (2008), an environmental writer for the *New York Times*, explained the difficulty of reporting on climate change, or any other complicated topic. In her words, "To get a story published reporters need to be able to present things as contro- versies, with two sides to every story." This means they seek balance and fairness, but that can itself be unfair. Boykoff and Boykoff (2004: 133) have argued, "[The] press's adherence to balance actually leads to biased coverage of global warming … This bias, hidden behind the veil of journalist balance, creates … political space for the U.S. government to shirk responsibility and delay action regarding global warming." Ross Gelbspan (2005a: 73), a former *Boston Globe* reporter, has written extensively about the media's coverage of global warming and gives them collectively a failing grade. He argues that it is a job of a reporter to first find out what the facts are and learn where the balance of scientific opinion lies. When reporters treat global warming as still a matter of conjecture, they have distorted the truth. An accurate balance would report that the vast majority of scientists, 95 percent-plus, are convinced humans have caused the planet to heat up and agree that the effects will be substantial and dire. Those who disagree, and they are few, would receive a paragraph at the end of the story.

State of Fear

In 2004 a number of books about climate change were published. Michael Crich- ton's, *State of Fear*, sold millions of copies and was a *New York Times Best Seller*. The novel is a thriller about a band of eco-terrorists, the Earth Liberation Front (ELF), who are trying to create a state of fear to advance their agenda about global warming. Their specialty is creating a series of "natural" disasters, one of which is to be a giant tsunami. However, our hero discovers the plot just in time, thwarts it and the ELF members are killed in a backwash of their own making. Crichton, himself a doctor and scientist, lards his book with footnotes that seem to back up claims that global warming is a fiction. Climate skeptics embraced the work but many scientists were sufficiently alarmed that several wrote articles and opinion columns expressing views, like those by Myles Allen (2005), head of the Climate Dynamics Group at the University of Oxford:

> Michael Crichton's latest blockbuster, *State of Fear*, is also on the theme of global warming and is likely to mislead the unwary … Although this is a work of fiction, Crichton's use of footnotes and appendices is clearly intended to give an impression of scientific authority.

President Bush invited Michael Crichton to the White House in 2005 to discuss the book, which alarmed a number of environmentalists. The American Association of Petroleum Geologists gave Crichton its 2006 Journalism Award, saying about the book, "It is fiction, but it has the absolute ring of truth" (Janofsky 2006). James Inhofe, United States Senator from Okalahoma who chaired the Senate Committee on Environment and Public Works from 2003–07, tried to make *Fear Factor* "required reading" for everyone on the committee. He had previously said, on the floor of the Senate, that "the threat of catastrophic global warming [is] the greatest hoax ever perpetrated on the American people."

Al Gore: An Inconvenient Truth

Al Gore, the 45th Vice President during Clinton's administration, was a strong supporter of the environment (1992). Under Clinton he pushed, unsuccessfully, for a **carbon tax** that would better reflect the true environmental costs of carbon-based fuels. He helped broker the 1997 Kyoto protocol, which would have committed the United States to reduce its greenhouse gases (GHGs) substantially. The U.S. Senate unanimously refused to endorse the agreement (95–0), which had been signed by many of the developed countries of the world, e.g., Japan, Germany, and Great Britain. Nevertheless Gore ran against George Bush in 2000 with a pledge that he would ratify the treaty. After Gore's defeat for the presidency, he focused on his long-standing interest in environmental issues. He gave a presentation around the country, which was concurrently released as both a book and a movie, *An Inconvenient Truth*. Gore described the causes of climate change, noted what its impacts would be, and called on people to take action. He framed his call to action in moral and spiritual terms.

> This … is a moral moment, a cross-roads. This is not ultimately about any scientific discussion or political dialogue. It is about who we are as human beings. It is

about our capacity to transcend our own limitations, to rise to this new occasion. To see with our hearts, as well as our heads, the response that is now called for. This is a moral, ethical, and spiritual challenge

(Gore 2006: 11)

The movie won numerous awards, including an Academy Award in 2006 for Best Documentary Feature. It had a definite impact. One poll reported that 69 percent of those who had watched the movie changed their minds about climate change and 74 percent said they had changed some behavior (e.g., recycling) as a result of watching the film (Nielsen 2007). In 2007, Al Gore received the Nobel Prize, along with members of the IPCC, for efforts to alert people to the dangers of climate change.

The scientific community lined up behind the movie noting that Gore had gotten it right (Borenstein 2006). That is, CO_2 was building up in the atmosphere; glaciers were melting; the Earth was warming; and there was no doubt but that humans had caused it. Other reactions to Gore's movie were varied and often negative. One reason is that Gore made it clear that climate deniers were driven by their own political and economic agendas. He was particularly distressed that President George Bush had rolled back and overturned many of the environmental initiatives of the Clinton administration, and distressed because Bush had hired Phillip Cooney to be in charge of environmental policy for the White House. Gore noted that Cooney had previously worked for the American Petroleum Institute and was head of a campaign to confuse the American people about global warming. Said Gore, "Even though Cooney has no scientific training whatsoever, he was empowered by the president to edit and censor the official assessments of global warming from the Environmental Protection Agency (EPA) and other parts of the federal government" (2006: 264). Cooney went so far as to edit out all mention of the dangers of global warming in EPA reports.

President George Bush said he had no intention of seeing the movie and suggested that instead of limiting greenhouse gases our energies would be better focused on the technologies that would allow us to live better lives and still protect the environment (Associated Press 2006). Even before the film's release, television ads ran with the support of the Competitive Enterprise Institute showing a little girl blowing the seeds off of a fluffy dandelion with the tagline, "Carbon dioxide. They call it pollution. We call it life" (*Grist* 2006).

Educators in the United Kingdom thought so highly of the movie that they wanted to make it part of their "Sustainable Schools Year of Action" and prepared to send copies to all secondary schools in England, Wales, and Scotland and make it part of the science curriculum for 4th- and 6th-year students. This decision was challenged by some parents who argued that the film was a form of illegal political indoctrination, because it supported the idea that humans were the cause of global warming. The ensuing court case found that there were a few mistakes in a movie with thousands of facts, but that it could be shown to students, *if* a teacher pointed out the minor errors.

It is important to underscore that there were two important messages that Gore was delivering. One was about the way we should live our lives and the obligations we have to future generations. Another was about the science that supported the points he was making. Both messages came under attack, although it was the science that received the greatest attention. It became the primary means by which people would try to discredit the idea that humans were causing a problem, because if humans were causing a problem, they would need to change their behavior and their lifestyles.

Campaigns of Deceit

If the movie *The Day After* was designed to entertain people and secondarily alert them to the issues surrounding climate change, *The Global Warming Swindle*, which aired as a documentary in the United Kingdom in March of 2007, left no doubt what its intentions were. Publicity for the film labeled global warming a scam, a lie, and the biggest hoax of all time. The film argued that research on global warming was deeply flawed, junk science, and that the consensus among climate scientists was simply due to their desire to get money for their research. It was a direct rebuttal to both the moral points and the scientific claims that Al Gore, among others, had been making. It also represented the globalization of the denial movement (Dunlap and McCright 2010).

The range of assertions made by the film was wide. Claims were made that water vapor makes up 95 percent of all greenhouse gases, and therefore has the greatest impact on the Earth's climate, not CO_2. Further, since the vapor forms clouds, which reflect heat, and scientists can't predict future weather patterns because of the clouds, then their models must be wrong. Carbon dioxide, it was argued, makes up only 0.5 percent of the Earth's atmosphere and human activity accounts for only 1 percent of that total. Some argued that the real cause of carbon dioxide build-up was dying leaves and decaying plants, all of which accounted for 100 times more CO_2 than humans contributed. Therefore, humans were not responsible for global warming.

In *The Global Warming Swindle*, it was argued that variations in solar activity (which we noted in Chapter I go in cycles) were currently at a high level, and this, along with cosmic rays that affected cloud formation, explained warming. Finally, in support of the arguments that warming could not have been caused by humans, it was noted that the Earth was warm before, during the Medieval Warm Period (AD 800–1300), which was followed by the Little Ice Age, and a period of warming and prosperity after that.

The Little Ice Age, which followed the warm period, is sometimes offered by non-scientists as an example that the Earth goes through natural cycles. We noted at the outset that, indeed, the Earth goes through natural cycles. But most of the scientists who write about the Little Ice Age take it as an example of the fact that the Earth's climate can swing between extremes very quickly; sometimes within people's lifetimes. Scott Mandia, a professor of physical sciences at the University of Suffolk, who has written about the period, is emphatic:

The current rate of global warming is unprecedented and is being caused by humans. *In no way can my summary of the research regarding the impact of regional climate change on the Viking civilization and Europe during the Little Ice Age be used to "prove" the current global warming is due to a natural cycle.*

(Mandia 2010: 1, emphasis added)

During the Little Ice Age, cold weather affected virtually everything: agriculture, health, economics, social strife, immigration, and is reflected in the art and literature of the time. How bad was it? Ladurie cites the journal of a priest from Angers in central France:

The cold began on January 6, 1709 and lasted in all its rigor until the twenty-fourth. The crops that had been sewn were all completely destroyed ... Most of the hens died of cold, as had the beasts in the stables. When any poultry did survive the cold, their combs were seen to freeze and fall off. Many birds, ducks, partridges, woodcock, and blackbirds died and were found on the roads and on the thick ice and frequent snow.

(Ladurie 1971, cited in Rosa and Deitz 1998: 43)

There were food riots in urban centers; Scots from the Highlands raided the cattle of those in the Lowlands; wine harvests plummeted; witch hunts took place, as people cast about for someone to blame; and people roamed abroad seeking food. In short, the Little Ice Age or climate change brought with it human disaster and rapid and uneven effects around the globe.

Scientific outrage against *The Global Warming Swindle* was substantial. The co-chair of the IPPC, John Houghton (2007), summarized the response of many when he said the program was "a mixture of truth, half truth and falsehood put together with the sole purpose of discrediting the science of global warming." The British Antarctic Survey (2007) challenged, among other claims made by the movie, the statement about volcanoes:

[T]he claim that human CO_2 emissions are small compared to natural emissions from volcanoes ... is untrue. [C]urrent annual emissions from fossil fuel burning and cement production are estimated to be 100 times greater than average annual volcanic emissions of CO_2.

(British Antarctic Survey 2007)

They added:

- The evidence for an unusual recent global warming is unequivocal, and is very likely due to human activity.
- Recent changes in solar activity bear no resemblance to temperature changes.

- Channel 4 (the British company that sponsored the film) used seriously flawed data—that solar flares were the cause of global warming—on which to base their program.

Houghton was more scathing in his criticisms of those who appeared on Channel 4.

> The most prominent person in the program was Lord Lawson, former Chancellor of the Exchequer, who is not a scientist and who shows little knowledge of the science but who is party to a conspiracy theory that questions the motives and integrity of the world scientific community.
>
> (Houghton 2007: 1)

It has recently been demonstrated that those who deny climate change lack the scientific expertise of those who do not deny it. William Anderegg and his colleagues at Stanford (2010) found that deniers had half as many publications as leading climate scientists, and that their papers were infrequently cited by other scientists. A close examination of the work of the top 100 climate scientists revealed that 97 percent of them believe that the Earth is warming and this is due to human activity. The public and the media simply do not know that some opinions are not grounded in reality. Anderegg gives an interesting response to the notion that climate scientists are all part of some giant conspiracy. He says, "If you were a young researcher and had the data to overturn any of the mainstream paradigms, or what the IPPC has done, you would become absolutely famous. Everyone wants to be the next Darwin, everyone wants to be the next Einstein."

Science does not occur in a vacuum. Science is affected by the political, economic, and social environment in which it finds itself. When the 15th century Polish astronomer, Copernicus, announced that it was the Sun, not the Earth, around which our planetary system revolved, he found himself under attack for heresy. The findings of science are readily embraced when they support existing ideologies. They are readily embraced when they solve a problem, such as a new vaccine that cures what was thought to be an incurable disease. Science was celebrated when the first manned space flight to the Moon occurred. We enjoy its benefits in numerous ways, from clean water to comfortable homes. We are proud when members of our universities and countries win Nobel prizes for their discoveries and breakthroughs that have made such things as cell phones, IPods, and computers ubiquitous, at least in the developed world. When science has given us so much, and promises more, why would people resist a finding on which the scientific community has achieved consensus: the Earth is warming and we are concentrating CO_2 in the atmosphere at such a dangerous level that the planet may be tipped out of ecological balance? Why don't people believe scientists or science? First, as the National Science Foundation (2004) has found, most Americans simply do not understand what science is; that it involves testing competing hypotheses, looking at *all* available data (confirming and non-confirming), and building up a body of verifiable facts about the way the world works. They do not understand that all science deals in probabilities and that when something has a high probability it does not mean that there is an equal and compelling reason to believe something else. Over two-thirds of Americans believe in pseudo-science (astrology, for example) and only 12 percent of adults can pass a 3rd-grade test on the science and technology of energy. Few know what the first two **laws of thermodynamics** are and why they even matter. We have already suggested other reasons why people do not credit climate science: they receive conflicting information and do not know who to trust. Often the information they do receive is only part of a story, or one crafted to deceive. People do not seek out alternative sources of information.

David Orr, one of America's most passionate and eloquent writers about the problems of global warming (2005: 46–48), has itemized the reasons he believes people do not understand what is at stake:

- The forces of denial are militant and brazen. People in high office have compared environmentalists and those who wish to save ecosystems to terrorists.
- The movement to have a habitable planet is challenged by the forces of capitalism that argue for perpetual economic expansion and an off-loading of our ecological costs onto others.
- Economic and religious fundamentalists have branded their fellow Americans, who believe in slowing economic growth and limiting carbon emissions, as evil.
- There has been an erosion of civil discourse and an erosion of our ability to solve problems collectively.

What this adds up to is *toxic discourse*, with one's enemies vilified; a situation where opponents play on people's fears rather than their compassion and sense of mutual obligation to one another; and to a *rejection* of science when it is about human health, improvement of the environment, and climate change (Orr 2009: 26) and an *acceptance* when it is about growth and profit. Climate change is an important topic with perceived winners and losers, which is partly what excites such passion and sometimes leads to a distortion of fact.

Political and Economic Battlefronts

Jacques, Dunlap, and Freeman (2008) examined 141 English language books to detail the themes that characterize the writings of environmental skeptics and to determine who funded, produced, and distributed the literature. What perplexed them was that polls consistently demonstrate that the U.S. public has traditionally supported environmental values and protection for the environment but more and more people are resisting taking action on climate change. They suggest that social conservatives have been able to capitalize on discussions of the environment to celebrate the ideology of the free market. They do so by challenging the importance of the issues and, as we read above, questioning the science behind calls to lower our carbon emissions. For skeptics, environmentalists are dangerous radicals.

Environmental skepticism is characterized by four overlapping themes:

- A rejection of scientific literature.
- The prioritization of other problems, i.e., the economy is more important.
- A free-market philosophy and pro-growth perspective.
- The view that environmentalism is a threat to progress.

If regulations are proposed, they must be based on "junk" science. If people propose that we consume less, they must be instigating a war on progress (McCright and Dunlap 2010).

Success in introducing such ideas into the mainstream of public discourse is due in large part to the creation of conservative think tanks (CTTs). CTTs had their origin in the 1970s, when businessmen funded them in opposition to what they saw as a culture of regulation and creeping government "socialism." When media leaders (print, television, and the Internet) seek to develop a "balanced" story, they turn to the CTTs for an alternative view. Among many groups, they now have the same legitimacy as mainstream scientists and academics. The CTTs downplay the importance of climate change, ozone depletion, loss of biodiversity, depletion of natural resources, pollution of the air and water, genetically modified organisms (GMOs), and exposure to toxic chemicals. The CTT, the American Policy Center, set its sights on Al Gore. John Meredith, policy director and one of its online experts, said,

> Al Gore wants to be God. Apparently, he will stop at nothing to advance his global warming agenda even though scientists in ever-increasing numbers are rejecting the unproven theory. One of the ways he wants to do it is by killing innocent Third World babies.

> (Americanpolicy.org 2007)

The reference to third-world babies derives from the idea that countries that are not yet developed will also need to control their growth and carbon emissions.

Who supports such organizations? The simple answer is: organizations that would benefit from the extraction and use of fossil fuels (Source Watch 2010). ExxonMobil, for instance, gave the National Center for Policy Analysis in Dallas Texas $75,000 in 2008, and the same year sent $50,000 to the Heritage Foundation, both of which are pro-growth and pro-oil (Adam 2009). The Heartland Institute, which announces on its website that "There is no consensus about the causes, effects, or future rate of global warming," has received more that $650,000 from ExxonMobil since 1998. The Scaife, Bradley, and Marshall foundations also have poured funds into CTTs. One of the more intriguing among them is the Oregon Institute of Science and Medicine, tucked away in the Siskiyou Mountains in Cave Junction, Oregon. It deserves attention, because a petition on its website is often offered as the "proof" that many scientists challenge the findings that the Earth is warming. A petition was sent in April of 1998 to tens of thousands of U.S. scientists and quickly made its way onto the Internet. The letterhead and the "scientific" paper ("The Environmental Effects of Increased Atmospheric Carbon Dioxide") that were enclosed were misleading. The paper claimed that CO_2 was a good thing; it helped plants grow and the more CO_2 in the atmosphere, the less water that leaves would lose, so plants could growth in drier conditions. All this led to the conclusion that industrial activities would lead to a greener planet and more biodiversity, not less.

> As coal, oil, and natural gas are used to feed and lift from poverty vast numbers of people across the globe, more CO_2 will be released into the atmosphere. This will help to maintain and improve the health, longevity, prosperity, and productivity of all people.
>
> (Robinson, Robinson, and Soon 2010)

It appeared that the petition was coming from the National Academy of Scientists and the paper had been published in the *Proceedings of the National Academy of Scientists*, a prestigious peer-reviewed publication. It had not, and the National Academy of Scientists sent out a news release noting, "The petition does not reflect the conclusions of the expert reports of the Academy." The Academy added that climate change was real and we need to take action to protect against dramatic changes. Many non-scientists have signed up to become deniers (http://www.oism.org).

In the early 1990s, when climate scientists started to suspect that coal and oil were changing the Earth's climate, Western Fuels, then a $400-million coal cooperative, spent $1 million to hire scientists who were climate skeptics, such as Robert Balling and S. Fred Singer, and send them around the country to "reposition global warming as a theory, not a fact" (Gelbspan 2005b). Through the Information Council on the Environment (ICE) the same group paid for advertising messages such as: "Who told you the Earth was Getting Warmer … Chicken Little?" And, "If the Earth is Getting Warmer, why is Minneapolis getting colder?"

The damage that such groups do is considerable (Oreskes and Conway 2010), because it casts doubt on serious science, because it drives a wedge between people, and because it limits the ability of governments to act on behalf of not only their own citizens, but also the citizens of other countries. Why act, when people aren't sure about the science? When, according to the Heartland Institute (2007), "All of the supposed catastrophic effects of global warming have been rebutted by scientists, including melting ice, hurricanes, other extreme weather, and extinction of wildlife." Let us examine a case where a state that understood the science committed to reductions, and where it understood the potentially devastating effects of climate change.

California as a Leader

In 2006 the Governor of California, Arnold Schwarzenegger, pushed for a reduction in California's greenhouse gas emissions, because rising sea levels, drought, and reduced water in reservoirs had the potential to wreck havoc on the economy of the state. The result was Assembly Bill 32 (AB 32). AB 32 was a bold initiative and would be fully enacted in 2012. The Bill recognizes that the United States is a major contributor worldwide to greenhouse gas emissions and that California, with its population of 37 million (or one in every eight Americans), is a major contributor to the nation's greenhouse gases. Although California has led the country in reduction of energy consumption per person, its population and energy needs keep growing. By 2020, California's population is projected to be 44 million people, making it the equal of some of the largest nations in the world. AB 32 requires the state not only to meet the needs of this expanding population but to roll back its greenhouse gas emissions from current levels. This challenge requires many different strategies. One was to require the utility companies in the state to increase their power grid "mix" to include 20 percent renewable energy, by 2010, from such sources as wind and solar farms and a mix of 33 percent by 2030. Another was to mandate higher fuel efficiency standards for cars, and filters for the many diesel pumps used to move water for agriculture, and filters for the diesel trucks moving freight up and down the state. The state requires all new government structures to meet high energy standards, and it is impossible for a California home owner to purchase anything other than an efficient air conditioning unit, unless they drive to another state. One advantage of these efforts, and a not insignificant one, is that the state mandates have helped to push forward the development of renewable energies, their incorporation into building designs, and the development of a "green" economy.

But partisan splits were growing and these would be mirrored on the national level (Baldassare, et al. 2009). In 2009, 76 percent of California Democrats believed that climate change was occurring, while only 34 percent of California Republicans did. Furthermore, 34 percent of the Republicans expressed the opinion that global warming would never happen. When we look outside California, the same situation has taken place: a decline overall in those who see climate change as a problem and growing partisan divides (Dunlap and McCright 2008). A 2010 PEW poll revealed a 40 percentage point gap between Democrats and Republicans with 75 percent of Democrats and 35 percent of Republicans indicating there is clear evidence of global warming. Furthermore, the number of Americans who believe the Earth is warming dropped substantially in three years from 77 percent down to 57 percent at the present time (PEW Research Centre 2010).

What could cause this shift—especially in light of the fact that there is mounting scientific evidence of climate change? The answer is: active opposition from some members of the business community; campaigns to discredit the science of global warming; and the change in economic circumstances.

The California Chamber of Commerce funded a study that claimed the bill would cost millions, jobs would be lost, and businesses would seek to locate elsewhere. A Stanford University energy expert, James Sweeney, said the conclusions reached by the study were "truly weird" (Kasler 2010). Nevertheless, it was argued that jobs and economic growth must take precedence over a focus on the environment and global warming. The challenge to AB 32, Propostion 23, was funded by the Howard Jarvis Taxpayers Association, two Texas oil companies, the Koch brothers from Wichita, Kansas, who have holdings in oil companies, as well as some California oil refiners and distributors. Venture capitalists poured money into the "green" economy in California and were pitted against those who sought to roll back curbs on GHGs. Proposition 23 was overwhelmingly defeated by California voters in November of 2010.

In early December of 2009, the EPA declared that gases produced by burning coal and oil were a danger to public health. In announcing the finding, Lisa Jackson, head of the EPA, gave the reasons. "Look at the droughts," she said, "the flooding, the changes in disease, the changes in migratory habits, the changes in our water cycle and climate" (Parsons and Tankersley 2009). By declaring greenhouse gases (carbon dioxide, methane, nitrous oxide, hydroflurocarbons) as pollutants, and therefore health hazards, the EPA opened the door for the federal regulation of power plants, as well as heavy industry and vehicles. Reaction was swift in coming. The U.S. Chamber of Commerce (2009) took the position that these rules would "lead to a command-and-control regime that will choke off growth by adding new mandates to virtually every major construction and renovation project." The National Association of Manufacturers (2009) said it would make "energy more expensive and force manufacturers to cut jobs … It will be a huge cost to the economy." The American Petroleum Industry claimed that President Obama was simply burnishing his credentials for the upcoming climate talks that took place in Copenhagen later in the year (December 2009), and added that the Clean Air Act was never meant to regulate greenhouse gases. The National Petrochemical & Refiners Association said the decision was based on "selective" science (Associated Press 2009). Finally, though it may not be the end of the story, in June, 2010, the Republican Senator from Alaska sought to pass a "disapproval resolution," arguing among other things that the EPA actions would wreck the economy. It was also a direct attack on the science behind the EPA's finding (Roberts 2010). The resolution failed on a close 53–47 vote.

The East Anglia Emails

Prior to the Copenhagen Climate Summit in 2009, somebody hacked into emails on the server at the University of East Anglia's Climate Research Unit in the United Kingdom, one of several units around the world that collect data on temperature. Among the 1,000 emails and 3,000 documents were exchanges between leading climate scientists, many of who served on the United Nations' Intergovernmental Panel on Climate Change. The emails showed scientists struggling to explain how to present their data, and emails expressing growing frustration at the time consumed by responding to requests for information under Britain's Freedom of Information Act. They also expressed dismay that research they regarded as flawed, and contrary to their own findings, had been published. The hacked emails and files were posted anonymously to the web, some believed with the intention of deliberately derailing coming December 2009 talks in Copenhagen, and to make it impossible to achieve global consensus on how to limit climate change. The furor surrounding the emails was intense, and some believed they had found the smoking gun that would disprove what scientists had been arguing for decades. Branded *Climategate*, some writers insisted that it "proved" scientists had been lying. The conservative columnist, Rich Lowry (2009: A19), took the opportunity to try to demonstrate that the skeptics were the real truth tellers. "In the climate debate, the self-professed advocates of 'science' have done everything they can to silence adverse opinions, declaring important questions about the history and future of climate 'settled' even though they are shot through with uncertainty." Letters to editors poured in denouncing climate science. "Oh boy, is the 'settled science' of global warming going unsettled," wrote a woman (Schumacher 2010: 6A) to her local newspaper. "Evidence of the fraud grows. So when are our schools going to present this evidence of a giant hoax?" She added for clarification, that the IPPC report on climate was a "massive effort to promote government takeover of society and fill Al Gore's pockets."

What did the emails reveal? The head of the research unit, Phil Jones, indicated that he had used a "trick" to hide the decline in average temperature. The so-called trick involved putting two different data sets together as Michael Mann at Pennsylvania State had done in a *Nature* article. For example, when we look at a curve of population growth over the centuries, it looks like a hockey stick with one notable exception. In the 1350s there is a slight downward dip, which corresponds with the Black Plague that took the lives of thousands. The one downward dip does not disprove the point that the world's population continues to grow at an unsustainable rate. Scientists cannot—as we said in Chapter I—look at a temperature reading from 1,000 years ago, because nobody then was measuring it. They use proxy data from tree rings and ice cores. Writers for *New Scientist* (2009: 16) carefully explained, "Raw data almost always has to be manipulated to correct for problems with the way measurements were made, or to reconcile measurements made in different ways."

Many scientists and professional organizations responded to *Climategate*. The IPCC noted that there was no conspiracy to hide data from the public or from climate deniers, "The body of evidence is the result of careful and painstaking work of hundreds of scientists worldwide." The American Geophysical Society noted that the emails were being used by contrarians to distort the scientific debate about global warming. The University of East Anglia investigated, as did other organizations, and all came to the same conclusion: the Earth is heating up and the data are there to prove it. Spring comes earlier, permafrost is melting, and ice shelves are breaking up, and so on.

Copenhagen

Given the extent of knowledge we have about climate change, why was an accord on emissions not reached? For one reason, political and economic self-interest were involved. Mohammad Al-Sabban, lead negotiator for Saudi Arabia, said that the hacked emails would have a huge impact because they demonstrated that climate change was not due to human activities (Black 2009). Mr. Al-Sabban believed that the Summit should be used to investigate climate science, which put him on the same plane as the U.S. Chamber of Commerce!

There was much hope and much to accomplish in Copenhagen. The Summit drew close to 45,000 people with different interests. There needed to be an agreement on emission targets for both developed and developing countries; there needed to be technology transfers so that developing countries could skip the stage of a carbon-based economy and go straight to a "green" economy; and a governance structure to assure compliance. Efforts to achieve a successor to the Kyoto protocol of 1997 were unsuccessful. The reasons are many, including the fact that some key governments, such as Saudi Arabia, did not want an agreement, and some developing countries did not want to have to limit their emissions at the very time they have begun to grow. David King, former chief scientific advisor to the United Kingdom government, summed it up:

> The failures of Copenhagen were the result of serious organizational issues, accompanied by glaring and often naive political errors. These included the destructive negativity of the NGOs [non-governmental organizations], that made unrealistic demands in terms of emission targets and aid and the Danish government's attempt to devise a climate agreement without the involvement of poorer nations.
>
> (King 2010: 3)

Confusion

We will return in Chapter IV to the question of what might work to reduce greenhouse gas emissions, as well as to address some of the other glaring problems faced by people throughout the world. In this chapter, we have explored the battle for public opinion, the ways in which people have tried to shape the climate-change debates, the attacks on science, and the reasons for them. One can reasonably conclude that ordinary citizens are confused about what the actual state of affairs is, and what they might do about it. In the next chapter, we will explore in detail how humans assess risk, how they make decisions, and why some messages are insufficient to motivate people to act and why, sometimes, they cause people to react in negative ways.

DISCUSSION QUESTIONS

1. Provide examples of how public opinion about climate change has been shaped, or is being shaped.
2. What has caused the topic of climate change to become politicized?
3. Why have there been deliberate campaigns of deceit to argue that climate change is not occurring, or if it is, that it is not caused by humans? Who funds such campaigns and why?
4. Why do some believe that science is just another ideology? What would be needed to change people's perceptions of science and to get them to trust the evidence about climate change?
5. What does David Orr see as the primary reasons people do not understand what is at stake in terms of climate change? What would you add to his list?

III: Calculating the Odds

How We Think about Risk and Climate Change

Many of us think we can beat the odds. Bad things happen to other people, not to us. But how do we calculate the odds? Sam C. Saunders (1996), a mathematics professor at Michigan State University, offers insight into how humans assess risk. There is a subtle difference between anticipated loss and a perceived loss. That is, we can't anticipate what we cannot perceive or imagine. We *perceive* that smoking cigarettes is addictive and shortens life expectancy. On *average*, the young person who starts smoking a pack of cigarettes a day when they are 20 is likely to die at 60, ten years earlier than the person who doesn't smoke (age 70). Basically, it means each time somebody lights up they are subtracting 20 minutes from their life expectancy. But what if the smoker knows somebody who smoked and lived until 80? The ***perceived* risk** to the young smoker is small; one more cigarette won't matter that hour, day, or week.

But, what if the ***anticipated* risk** were different? What if, among all the packages sold daily, there would be a few cigarettes that would explode and blow the head or hand off the person holding the cigarette? People might calculate the risks differently. Saunders asks us to assume for the sake of argument that cigarettes are not harmful except for the one cigarette, among all the others, that explodes. The result, with 30 million packages sold and smoked daily, would be 1,600 daily deaths or disfigurements, higher than the number of people killed daily in automobiles. But this number would still be lower than the people who actually die *each day* from smoking-related diseases such as lung cancer. The *anticipated* risk as opposed to the *perceived* risk would probably cause a number of people either to give up smoking or not start. Many find it hard to think about climate change, because it is a perceived risk, something that will occur in the future, and something that is different from what we experience on a daily basis. It is also, as we learned in Chapter II, that some organizations and individuals are actively involved in an attempt to shift people's attention away from the anticipated risks of climate change.

Manufacturing Dissent

There are parallels between campaigns to discredit climate science and the campaigns that tobacco companies mounted (Dunlap and McCright 2010). Tobacco companies still work hard to shift people's attention away from anticipated risks and instead focus on short-term benefits—it's a way to take a break in a hectic world, to socialize with your friends, or to project an image of being a risk taker. For years, tobacco companies fought to suppress information that smoking was bad for your health and paid for "research" to demonstrate that second-hand smoke was not hazardous (Michaels 2008; Oreskes and Conway 2010). Lobbyists were hired to walk the halls of Congress to block legislation to regulate the sale and use of tobacco. They presented results from their "scientists" to challenge studies that showed a link between smoking and cancer. Smokers themselves fought attempts to block smoking in restaurants, bars, and public places, claiming that it was an infringement of their personal freedom to be denied the right to light up. One of the reasons that anti-smoking campaigns were successful, and why there are warning labels on every package of cigarettes sold, is that most of us knew about somebody who had died of a smoking-related disease. We could actually see how tobacco affected people's lives. But few of us have yet seen the direct effects of climate change. By framing the issue of climate change as a challenge to our individual rights and freedoms, attention is shifted away from the fact that this is a problem that requires collective solutions. Yet, framing the issue of climate change in such a way that it challenges the way we live is necessary, because no one really wants to experience its direct effects.

Competing Narratives

Former Vice President Gore titled his book and movie about climate change *An Inconvenient Truth*. "The truth about climate change is an inconvenient one *that means we are going to have to change the way we live our lives*" (2006: 286, emphasis added). For climate skeptics such as Philip V. Brennan (2009), this statement revealed the real purpose behind the global climate movement, which was "the establishment of a world socialist order under the control of the United Nations." Brennan urged his readers to fight this takeover with the same vigor with which we had fought the Cold War.

Gore has continued to challenge those who deny the fact that the climate is changing. As he said recently (2010: 11), "We can't just wish away climate change." He added that a great burden would be lifted if we could do so, because "we would no longer have to worry that our grandchildren would one day look back on us as a criminal generation that had selfishly and blithely ignored clear warning that their fate was in our hands." In short, Gore sees climate change as a *moral* challenge, as well as a challenge to our economic and political system.

Dennis Soron (2010: 78) has noted that many conservative politicians and business leaders in the advanced financial capitals of the world (New York, London, and Tokyo) "have long regarded environmental politics as a clandestine means of repackaging socialist goals and foisting them upon an unsuspecting public." Others see the topic of climate change as a serious challenge to contemporary capitalism. Brenda Longfellow notes that the climate crisis

> implicates energy regimes, models of development, how we organize cities, suburbs and transportation systems, public utilities and private corporations. It crosses issues of social justice in the global South and the crisis of democracy just about everywhere, and it puts the future on the agenda for all of us.
>
> (Longfellow 2006: 1)

Once we say that climate change and its solutions depend on sharing resources more widely, dealing with problems of global inequality, taking into account future generations, and changing our consumption habits, the conversation shifts dramatically. It shifts from a discussion about the science of global warming to a much broader discussion about basic human rights and what all people need to live decent lives. Some see this as an opportunity, while others see it as a challenge to their ideologies and world views, not to speak of their comfort.

World Views

World views are all-encompassing systems that allow us to make sense of our past, present, and future. All cultures have creation stories, explaining the unseen and unknown. Some have world views that emphasize cooperation, community, modesty, and humility, sharing of resources, respect for elders, and the need to co-exist with the natural world. On the other hand, there are creation stories that can be interpreted to support the individual over the group, the domination of the natural world, and the acquisition of material goods. Our world views (religious, political, economic, and social) are shaped by the culture and history we inherit, as well as the world we actively create through our daily actions. Climate change, as a world view, is part of an emerging discussion about how we *should* live our lives, what our relationship to one another *should* be, and what our relationship *should* be to future generations. It is a discussion that encompasses how to balance economic, social, and environmental needs across the entire planet. In this sense, climate change can be seen as a world view.

That is one of the reasons why the *science of climate change* provokes such strong reactions; some see it as a new form of religion, economics, or politics. I want to emphasize that climate change is *first and foremost a description of a changing physical reality*. However, as Mike Hulme (2009), a leading climate scientist, has noted, our current discussions about climate change reveal some deeply held but different assumptions about how we make sense of climate change and what we think is possible. How we think about problems often shapes what we think the solution to the problem should be.

Many discussions by environmentalists about climate change express first and foremost a sense of loss; a loss of such things as open space, clean air and water, and the sense of community that is sometimes associated with unspoiled landscapes and small communities. Here we have the notion that the solution to climate change lies in returning to an *Edenic past*, a more simple time and an ecologically unspoiled place. Many of you saw the very popular 2009 movie, *Avatar*, which takes place in the year 2154 on Pandora, a distant planet in the Alpha Centauri star system. The Na'vi, are a ten-foot-tall, blue-skinned species who live in harmony with nature, worshiping a mother goddess. Unfortunately for the Na'vi, their dwelling, Hometree, sits on top of massive deposits of *unobtanium*. The evil RDA corporation (an interplanetary mining company that seeks out scarce resources needed on their home planet) is intent on securing this valuable resource and eliminating the Na'vi if necessary. A great battle ensues with the RDA bringing in massive gunships and explosives to destroy the Na'vi's home. In the end (although two sequels are planned), the Na'vi triumph. Some audience members reported they were depressed after seeing the movie because they wanted to live on a place like Pandora—a place that does not exist.

Though a focus on the environment is critical to understanding our fragile world, this world view also has some limits, if taken to an extreme. An exclusive focus on the environment does not allow us to solve the larger problem. It cannot. No matter what we do, the Earth will warm for another 100 years, even if we stop emitting CO_2 and methane today. These gases do not respect community boundaries, let alone national boundaries. No one has the option of moving to Pandora.

A second perspective, the *apocalyptic*, or the end of the world, leads to a belief that individuals can do nothing to stop it. A third perspective claims *humans are creative* so we can solve any problem that comes our way. Such a perspective leads, as we will see, to suggestions that we geo-engineer the planet to ward off climate change. It assumes we are still at war with the natural world. This final perspective also assumes that *the* problem to solve is climate change but, as we have seen, climate change is tightly linked to problems of population growth, global inequality, water shortages, and the destruction of Earth's ecosystems. Hulme (2009) suggests that the topic of climate change be used to think about the very idea of the human condition. He's right, but do we have time to do that?

John Holdren (2009), President Obama's science advisor, has said that we are experiencing rapid climate change and that a rise in global average surface temperature (which would happen in about 90 years) would be an absolute catastrophe. Rajendra Chaudhaury, who is chair of the Intergovernmental Panel on Climate Change (IPPC), said in 2009 that we have only six years to limit peak emissions before we are faced with devastating changes. David Orr (2009: 183–84), who has written extensively about climate change, argues that we are facing a global emergency and playing the equivalent of Russian roulette with the Earth. We are down to the wire with no time to waste. This is why so many who write about climate change do so in moral terms.

Moral Framing

Eban Goodstein, a professor of economics at Lewis and Clark College in Portland, Oregon, explains why he cares about global warming:

> Where I live, in Oregon, global heating is going to cut the summer water supply in our streams and rivers by half, condemning my children to year after year of summer drought. Unchecked global heating will kill more people and drive more animals to extinction than has any industrial pollutant in human history. I think that's really wrong. Don't you?
>
> (Goodstein 2007: 81–82)

The language of right and wrong can be used to frame discussions about climate change. Goodstein argues that we must use the language of morality in order to help people realize the dangers we are facing and the obligations we have to one another.

> We absolutely need to talk about values, our focus needs to be on right and wrong policies, not right and wrong people. Government—our collective voices—consistently has made the wrong moral choices, subsidizing big fossil fuel producers.
>
> (Goodstein 2007: 81)

David Orr (2009: 197) is equally emphatic in his view that the way in which we are collectively living our lives in the developed countries of the Western world is wrong. It is wrong, in his view, because we have a model of economic growth based on consumption and the depletion of natural resources instead of one focused on the improvement of the quality of life for everyone. It is wrong because we are focused on meeting our wants, not our needs, while hundreds of millions of people go to bed hungry every night. It is wrong because we must do a better job of distributing in a fair manner risk, opportunity, and wealth. For many, climate change is a story about modernity itself, carrying with it "an indictment of consumerism, industrialization, corporatism and globalization" (Clarke 2010: 308).

The reality is that most of us frame problems in terms of the language (religious, political, environmental) we have available and, again, that language is shaped by our own personal and cultural experiences. One way to frame the issue of climate change is Biblical: "*Thou shalt not steal.*" Therefore, it is wrong to steal from future generations. One can frame the discussion in terms of our sense of stewardship and obligation to protect what we understand to be the gifts of the Creator, or we can frame the issue, as some do, from a perspective claiming we are superior to all other creatures, who are here on Earth to meet our needs. You could also see climate change as a wedge for a socialist agenda. However, what science demands is a framing of the discussion in terms of basic scientific principles (Orr 2009: 192).

- *The laws of thermodynamics*: e.g., matter can neither be created nor destroyed and all systems tend to entropy.
- *The idea of **carrying capacity***: there is a finite limit to the number of species that the environment can sustain indefinitely.
- Earth's biological and ecological systems are connected *in one complex system.*

As much as we might want to wish away the laws of science and the facts, we cannot. We have seen, though, that when the facts of science are used to make moral arguments, it is difficult to develop clear and common understandings of what must be done. Some ways of framing an issue can help to mobilize people to solve a problem; other ways of framing can cause people to freeze in fear, or lash out in anger. Some ways of framing simply obscure the nature of the problems we are facing.

Climate Change, Religion, and Creationism

We find ourselves today in an unusual situation in which science is seen by some people as just another ideology. Since Darwin published *The Origin of Species* in 1859, many people have seen religion and science as opposed to one another. Yet for most of the 20th century there was an understanding that there are two separate spheres—one grounded in faith and one grounded in fact—which could coexist. However, we have witnessed the active erosion of this understanding. One reason is the resurgence of conservative religious groups that have chosen to support specific economic, political, and social arrangements and the political candidates who favor those arrangements. This is a subtle shift from religion being a matter of faith to religion being a matter of ideology. The news of climate change does not fit a model that argues for a creationist view of the world. Science is seen, then, as a challenge to a world view and to an ideology. Evolution is seen as just another "theory" which should be taught as such. Climate change is simply another theory to be challenged or—in some cases—seen as God's plan. It is essential that public policy that affects our collective welfare be informed by science, but when science seems to support one set of policies over another (we need to lower our greenhouse gas emissions now) some have come to see science as just one more option in a wide range of choices.

Climate change, then, can be framed in many different ways: 1) as a technical problem for which we can find solutions; 2) as a problem endemic to capitalism because of its emphasis on consumption and continued growth; 3) as a problem of conflicting values; 4) or, it can be framed as a national security problem. The U.S. Navy (Greenert 2010) sees climate change as a reality for which the military must prepare. It will weaken governments in Africa, as food security and water security become ever greater issues. It can lead to mass migrations as millions of people flee unstable regimes seeking food and water, and it will threaten our own island military bases, because of rising sea levels.

If many agree on the nature of the problem, the science is clear on the overall trends, and the implications are dramatic, why don't people change their behavior and use fewer resources or help others in need? Why does it seem as though we don't care about the future?

Climate Change by the Numbers

The Milky Way galaxy contains 200 billion stars and there are 200 billion other galaxies in the universe. Life has evolved over roughly four billion years. If you live to be 100 you will have lived for about ¼₀ th billion of the time life has existed on Earth. But never underestimate your impact. In the United States we send six billion tons of CO_2 into the atmosphere every year. Your share is more than 20 tons each year. What, exactly, are we to make of these numbers? The answer posed by Cole (1998: 17) is not much. "Our brains, it appears, may not be engineered to cope with extremely large or small numbers." So, we search for ways to make numbers large and small meaningful. Consider your 20 tons of carbon dioxide (or 40,000 lb) a year. If you weighed as much as 200 lb, you would have produced 200 people who weighed as much as you, occupying space on the planet. Does CO_2 actually weigh something? For numbers to have meaning to us, they need to have a human "face" or dimension, otherwise they are just a bunch of zeros. The average American household takes on average 12 trips a day by car. Really. This is going and coming to work, running back to the pharmacy, going to the grocery store, going to meet a friend, and all of the many things we do without thinking about it.

If you drive a car, or ride in one, when you fill up with a gallon of regular unleaded gasoline that one gallon weighs about 6.3 lb. After you've driven however far your car gets you on one gallon of gasoline, you have added 20 lb of CO_2 to the atmosphere. The weight comes from the oxygen already present in the air. When gasoline, which is 87 percent carbon, burns, it separates into carbon and hydrogen. The hydrogen forms with oxygen to form water, H_2O (which is why you sometimes see drips of water coming from your exhaust). The 5.5 lb of carbon in your gallon of fuel combines with oxygen and it forms CO_2. A carbon atom has a weight of 12 and oxygen has a weight of 16, which means that each molecule of CO_2 has an atomic weight of 44 (12 + 16 + 16). The result is that *6.3 lb of gasoline becomes 20 lb of CO_2* (United States Department of Energy and Environmental Protection Agency 2010).

The little things we do make a big difference but often we are completely unaware that they do. There are few of us, however, who calculate our impact on the planet when we act; and there are even fewer who shape their behavior in terms of hard-to-imagine changes of how we are used to living.

Assessing Risk

Daniel Kahneman and Amos Tversky (1979) pioneered the field of behavioral economics by showing there is a mathematical and empirical basis (**prospect theory**) to how human beings assess risk. They were among the first to show that we consistently think we will beat the odds, because we are special. "I won't get arrested for drunk driving, because I'm not that drunk and I'm a good driver." We think if something has not happened before, it's not likely to happen in the future, but failing to buckle your seat belt because you are just going to the grocery store can result in tragedy. Events of low probability, or what we think of as a low probability, are given a probability of zero. But repeatedly playing Russian roulette can only have one outcome (Bernstein 1996).

In a confusing world, we look for what Kahneman and Tversky refer to as **anchors**, which is a cognitive bias in favor of what we already know, which can be just one piece of information. How the information is delivered, or framed, often leads to the choice we make. Would you rather go to the gym every week and work out to improve your health and gain control of your weight or would you like to take this pill that will help you "burn fat"? Tversky and Kahneman (1974) told people to imagine there was a rare disease that would kill 600 people. They were then asked to choose between two options. The first, strategy A, would save 200 people; the second, strategy B, would kill 400. The results are exactly the same, of course, but people uniformly choose A. We choose the good news over the bad, or use the very first piece of information we get to make decisions about how we handle related information. If we hear that the effort to reduce CO_2 emissions will wreck the economy, and that information comes from family and friends, that is likely to be sufficient for us. This represents what social scientists refer as a **confirmation bias**. We seek out information that supports our positions, not information that undermines it. We find this information from people who are like us, with whom we associate because they have the same ideas as we do. We do not seek out information that runs contrary to our established opinions.

Closely related to confirmation bias is the **Dunning–Kruger effect**. People who don't *know* much, don't know they don't know much, and hence don't seek additional information (Surowiecki 2010). One refrain that continues to echo from the Republican national campaign of 2008 was "Drill, baby, drill!" The implication was that somehow, someone, somewhere, was responsible for the high price of gas, but not the oil companies. It was suggested that we could meet our energy needs if we drilled in the Alaskan National Wildlife Refuge (ANWR). ANWR is 19 million acres, the largest protected wilderness area in the United States. It is one of the richest sites for biological diversity and life in North America. How much oil is actually there, and would it really make a difference? Recall that the CIA reports that we use close to seven billion barrels of oil a year. The U.S. Geological Survey, which is responsible for the accounting of natural resources, estimates that there might be as many as 16 billion barrels of oil available in ANWR, but emphasizes that only about half this amount is likely to be recovered. The oil is indeed valuable but it represents only a little over one year's worth of our needs. Is it worth drilling for that when the environmental costs are estimated to be staggering?

We have a strong tendency to choose immediate benefits, even though they are small, over significant long-term benefits (Lea 2010). And, coupled with this, we engage in **relative thinking**. If we do not have more of something (our house has increased in value instead of declining in value) we tend not to be happy. *We fear loss more than we value gain*. We fear the current economic crisis, because we know somebody who has been affected or because we fear we might be. Most of us have not been impacted, but the fear outweighs the willingness to do with less, or to help those who have actually been impacted. We resist making investments in the planet now, because we do not see an immediate gain.

We make many of our decisions based on our illusions, on the exotic, on the things that occur only infrequently. In one study (Schkade and Kahneman 1998) Midwesterners and Californians were asked whether or not living in California was likely to make people happy. Both groups said Californians were more likely to be happy, because they lived in California, even though both groups scored the same on a happiness scale. In other words, California is an exotic place where everyone must be happy. The number of people who believe they can be made happy by moving to California has made it the largest (37 million) state in the nation.

We protect our children by driving them to school so they won't be kidnapped by strangers. Yet the data make it very clear that if children are abducted or harmed, it is likely to be by a family member or by a friend. We tend to guard against things that are not likely to happen, while ignoring those that are.

Climate change is scary. It ought to be because the potential consequences, even though they all might not happen during your lifetime, are great. But, fear, despair, and a sense of being overwhelmed can lead to inaction. Citing the work of Moser and Dilling (2004), Swim and her colleagues note that

> well-meaning attempts to create urgency about climate change by appealing to fear of disasters or health risks frequently lead to the act opposite of the desired response: denial, paralysis, apathy, or actions that can create greater risks than the one being mitigated.
>
> (Swim, et al. 2009: 80)

The emotional effects of disasters on people should not be underestimated but the emotional, as well as the physical, impacts very greatly depending on people's resources. The aftermath of Hurricane Katrina has been well documented. Many people simply did not have the economic resources to try and rebuild their homes; they were left with literally nothing. Sometimes in disasters (Solnit 2009) people behave heroically, rebuilding their communities and lives with fierce determination; sometimes the disaster is so great they cannot. Whatever the impact is, be it a drought, hurricane, withering summer heat, it is mediated through social networks. The impact of an extended heat wave or freezing temperatures for most of us who live on the North American continent is small; for now, at least, we have the power to adjust the thermostat. On a global scale the different ways that people have to cope with climate change are substantial. Some can pool resources; some can draw on the knowledge of experts; and some must suffer. This is no different from the way in which we cope with a financial downturn: we may borrow money; move in with friends or family; draw on our savings; take on extra work; or do with less. Whether or not we think something is a risk depends a lot on how many resources we have.

We can also simply deny that a problem even exists. The American Psychological Association (Swim, et al. 2009: 80–90) summarized the many ways in which psychology could contribute to an understanding of how we think about global warming. The authors of the report noted that our emotions range widely. We can:

- Deny it is happening.
- *Reason* it is happening but *there is nothing we can do about it.*
- Engage with our emotions and *justify our actions*, by claiming what we do does not help.
- Stave off anxiety by *increasing our consumption*, under the misguided assumption that money might buy happiness (Lea 2010).
- *Shop "green"* under the assumption that buying organic cotton t-shirts, or other products, will save the planet (Szasz 2008).
- *Take action* and work to solve the problem.

But there are barriers that stand between us and choosing what to do. First, we might not do anything because *we do not know there is even a problem.* How would you know, unless you had made an effort to find out, that Yemen may be the first country in the world to run out of water? Sandra Steingraber (2008) refers to our failure to understand what is going on in the biosphere, or even in our own backyards, as **environmental amnesia**. We spend our time in malls, locked up in schools, houses and office buildings, paying little attention to what goes on in the environment on which our lives depend. We know and are concerned about hazardous materials, pesticides used on the fruit we eat, and Bisphenol A in plastic water bottles. Steingraber gave a lecture in Rockford, Illinois, about toxic chemicals. Rockford is a Superfund clean-up site because, among other reasons, toxic solvents were released over the years into the water table. The well water that people used was so toxic that simply taking a shower was poisonous. When she told her audience about these things only two members of the audience even knew. In northern California, people love to fish in the Feather River, catching trout, occasionally salmon, and other fish. Yet, very few fishermen know that the fish they catch and eat are dangerous to their health because of polychlorinated biphenyls (PCBs) that have accumulated in the tissue of fish, having leached into the water from illegal dumping. Most do not *want* to know.

Second, *many people do not trust the experts*, or do not even know what would qualify one as an expert in climate science. Third, we may think it is *somebody else's job to act*, such as the government, or the people who we believe are responsible for a drought. Wasn't it the fault of the Ethiopians that they were starving because they had so degraded the environment that crops could not be raised, or there were simply too many of them because they had not limited the growth of their populations? Fourth, we could not act because *we think what we do will make no difference*. Does it really matter to the health of the planet if I drink water from plastic bottles and throw them in the trash instead of using a refillable container?

We are "hard-wired" to respond to risk in terms of our emotions, not our analytical reasoning skills. In terms of the development of our brains and dietary needs we are still stuck in the Paleolithic Era (Stone, Bronze, and Iron Ages), which constitutes about 99 percent of human history. It made good sense, evolutionarily, for us to be able to respond to immediate and obvious threats. If something with big teeth was charging us, our brains probably said, "Run!" Modern society, however, asks that we think problems through in a more rational and deliberate manner. But, we have not yet abandoned our old ways of thinking and responding. A good response requires both emotion and reason. As Slovic and his colleagues (Slovic, et al. 2004) have noted, even intelligent people cannot understand and respond to the simplest of numbers— unless those numbers are infused with meaning or feeling. For example, the simple fact that 115 people die every day, or one every 13 minutes, from traffic accidents, is not likely to affect our driving decisions. It might if we knew somebody who had been killed. That is why some campaigns about climate change appeal to us through pictures of polar bears clinging to pieces of ice, or brown pelicans covered with oil. We need feelings so we can act.

Acting rationally is not easy to do if we are given abstract representations of the future. We sort things out in terms of our immediate and perceived risks, which are heavily influenced by the everyday world of habit. William James, the great psychologist, once described habit as the "enormous flywheel of society." We keep doing what we have been doing, because it works, at least for us, if not for people in other parts of the world. Thus, when asked to be "green" to make a change that might make a difference for future generations we want to know such things as:

- Will it work?
- Is it safe?
- Will it cost me money?
- Is there a social risk?

There are obvious economic barriers to, for example, putting up a windmill in the backyard or erecting a solar field to power your dwelling. (There may also be legal barriers.) But cultural and social barriers are important too. Our cultures have a powerful influence on our consumption behaviors and on the things we do to minimize risk in our lives, and these things change over time. Whether or not you believe a microwave oven or a plasma-screen television is a necessity obviously depends on *your personal meaning of what constitutes quality of life.* More U.S. citizens every year have come to believe that dishwashers, cell phones, computers, cars, boats, and new clothes are essential to their well-being; these things are defined as meeting essential needs, not just luxuries. Yet the person picking through a garbage dump in Mumbai, India, scavenging what others throw away, is trying to make a life.

On any given day there are many things that can consume our attention. Psychologically there are a limited number of things we can worry about at any given time. In 2010, people were asked about the things that worried them (PEW). On a list containing 21 items, global warming came in last (28 percent) on a list of top priorities for those living in the United States. It is no surprise that the economy (83 percent) and jobs (81 percent) topped the list, given the economic downturn. Other priority concerns were terrorism (80 percent) followed by social security (66 percent), education (65 percent), and health care (57 percent).

In wanting to live risk-free lives, protect our families, avoid social ridicule, and maintain what we think of as quality lives, we ignore greater long-term risks. We are numb to numbers. We are driven by emotions, which can be swayed as easily by those who believe existing social relationships are acceptable, as by those who believe they are not. For those who believe that somehow the economic markets can sort things out, it is well to consider just how poor some large organizations are when it comes to assessing risk, as they are focused on immediate gains. Naomi Klein (2010) has written about the devastating effect of the BP oil spill in the spring and summer of 2010. She reports that BP believed it was inconceivable (because it had not happened before) that the blowout preventer would fail, so there was no back-up plan. The plans submitted by BP to government regulators for the Deepwater Horizon rig make frequent use of the term, "little risk," and note that the company is using "proven technology." And, even if a spill were to occur, there would be "little risk of contact or impact to the coastline." We know, of course, that the risks were extreme and the long-term environmental, economic, and social costs are incalculable. Stopping drilling in the Gulf of Mexico will not even be considered, because there are 35,000 jobs that depend on oil and gas exploration in the Gulf and over 30 percent of this country's domestic supply of oil comes from the Gulf.

Acting Responsibly

The United States has a unique responsibility to act to limit the build-up of carbon in the atmosphere. We are but 5 percent of the world's population, using 25 percent of the world's oil every year. We are responsible, on a per capita basis, for more CO_2 going into the atmosphere than any other nation. Climate change is real; it will have disastrous consequences; and we must act. For people to act they have to both know the problem is real and they have to understand it is in their self-interest to act. Not acting will lead to floods, hurricanes, droughts, disease, and economic collapse (Meyerhoff 2008). Acting will protect people's homes, families, children, and grandchildren. In the next chapter, we will discuss some of the things that people can do as individuals and things that must be done by governments.

DISCUSSION QUESTIONS

1. Are there similarities between the campaigns that sought to convince people that smoking was not bad for your health and current campaigns that seek to convince people that climate change is not real or is not caused by humans?
2. Provide examples of how humans assess risk and explain how this relates to taking action to address issues of global warming.
3. Is fear an effective way to communicate the dangers of climate change and spur people to act? What would be effective and what would lead to action?
4. What are the different ways in which we can frame or understand climate change? Which is likely to be most effective in getting people to act?
5. How does the concept of environmental amnesia help us to understand why we do or do not act? What would be a good way (or ways) to help people overcome their environmental amnesia and get them to act?

IV: What is the Future Worth?

$\sim\!\!\sim\!\!\times\!\!\sim$

Each of our lives—through the numerous choices we make daily—affects the climate and has a role in creating the future. Yet these connections are often invisible. If we cannot see the consequences of our actions, how can we change?

What is the real price of a gallon of gasoline? If you paid the full cost for a gallon of regular gas you should pay at least $10.84 (Kimbrell, et al. 1998).[1] The average retail price of, say, around $3.00 hides costs you pay elsewhere and costs that fall on others, including future generations.

How often do you think of the taxes you pay for the oil companies? The Federal government provides numerous tax breaks to oil companies so they can compete with international producers. They can take the immediate expense of exploration and recovery costs off of their total tax bill. They are allowed accelerated depreciation allowances, and provided foreign tax credits, and foreign income deferrals (United States Energy Information Administration 2010). These may all be good policies to assure a supply of cheap oil, but they mean that you pay more taxes while others pay less.

A gallon of gasoline has many **external costs** that neither the oil companies nor the consumer pays. An external cost is a consequence of an economic activity that is experienced by unrelated third parties. It usually is not accounted for in the retail price (Levitt and Dubner 2009). The military helps protect oil supplies. Burning gasoline contributes to global warming, localized air pollution, and associated health risks. Gasoline powered cars allow people to drive long distances, and contribute to urban sprawl. Local and regional governments pay for the infrastructure (sewer, water, roads) that supports suburbs. Municipalities pay for keeping ice off roads in the winter and— along with state and federal governments—for repairing and upgrading them. Roads degrade ecosystems. And it goes on.

---

1   The authors detail how the real cost of gasoline is computed. They provide both a high and low estimate of cost; I have chosen the median price and stated that price in current dollars. It is also important to know that when the authors gave their projection, oil was selling for less than $20 a barrel. Therefore, my figure of $10.84 is low.

Tragedy of the Commons

The number of negative externalities is substantial. When we take a bite of a hamburger from a fast food restaurant, we do not think we are eating oil. Yet oil went into its production and into the fuel for the trucks, trains, or ships that transported the meat. Tractors running on gasoline or diesel plowed the ground to grow the grain to feed to the cattle. Petroleum-based products fertilized the grain. Trees may have been cut down in the Amazonian rainforest to clear the land for grazing the cattle. Those who serve us, maintain the restaurant, and grow, harvest, and manufacture the ingredients for the bun, sauce, and packaging may not receive a living wage. We do not pay for the environmental degradation, the use of scarce and irreplaceable resources, or the workers' diminished quality of life.

Garrett Hardin (1968) described a major problem—the **tragedy of the commons**—that confronts us today. He noted that overgrazing was a feature of community pastures (commons) in Medieval Europe. The "tragedy" was that by seeking to maximize his individual gains each herder degraded the commons and eventually everyone was worse off. Each herder acted rationally, in the sense that every extra cow he grazed provided him with direct benefits, but the result was that the loss or externality (degraded pasture) was shared by all herders. Hardin offered this as a cautionary tale for modern society, in which we share such commons as the atmosphere, oceans, rivers, fish stocks, and national parks. His work has been used to help people understand the fundamental concept of sustainability: we must work together to balance environmental, economic, and social needs.

What Kind of a Problem are we Trying to Solve?

Climate change has been described as a **"wicked" problem** for which clumsy solutions are sometimes offered (Prins and Rayner 2007; Prins, et al. 2010; Rayner 2006). It is a "wicked" problem because it comprises several problems that are closely tied together; a change in one triggers a change in the others, sometimes with unknown results. Melting Arctic ice, for example, reduces the reflective properties (albedo effect) of ice, which in turn causes the temperature to rise and more ice to melt. Prins and his colleagues noted that:

> Rather than being a discrete problem to be solved, climate change is better understood as a persistent condition that must be coped with, and can only be partially managed more—or less—well. It is just one part of a complex of such conditions encompassing population, technology, wealth disparities, resource use, etc. Hence, it is not a straight-forward environmental problem. It is axiomatically as much an energy problem, an economic development problem or a land-use problem, and

may be better approached through these avenues than as a problem of managing the behavior of the Earth's climate by changing the way humans use energy.

(Prins, et al. 2010: 16)

Prins and Rayer (2007) offered the example of the cartoon, *Wallace and Gromit*. In the episode of the "Wrong Trousers" the boy Wallace put on a pair of robotic pants thinking they would make walking his dog, Gromit, easier. The trouble was the pants took Wallace to places he had never imagined. We put on the wrong trousers in Copenhagen when we assumed scores of nations could get together and agree on limits, as they did when they got together to ban the use of CFCs, which were creating a hole in the ozone layer (*Economist* 2009). In the case of the ozone layer, people agreed on the problem, understanding that if things were not fixed, there would be health consequences. In addition, a readily available substitute existed at a comparable price. In Copenhagen, governments were asked to do something they had not done before, "exercise restraint for altruistic reasons" (*Economist* 2009: 10).

When nuclear weapons were controlled by the two superpowers (the Soviet Union and the United States), they sat down and hammered out an agreement (the Strategic Arms Reduction Treaty, START). Yet, at that time, they were virtually the only two countries with nuclear weapons and it was in the interests of both economically and strategically to limit the arms race. All countries, though, are impacted by climate change and have different problems to solve.

What are the Problems to be Solved?

As a wicked problem, rapid climate change involves numerous interconnected problems. Lester Brown (2009: 23–24) believes there are four critical problems we must address to maintain food security and sustain civilization:

- Reduce CO_2 emissions from current levels by 80 percent by 2020.
- Stabilize the world's population, projected to grow to nine billion by 2050, at eight billion or lower.
- Restore Earth's natural systems, including forests, aquifers, grasslands, and fisheries.
- Eradicate poverty.

Brown's list is a good one, though daunting. But the solutions that have been proposed to deal with such problems vary greatly, because people have more than one view of human nature. Believing human beings are adaptable, creative, and committed to helping one another yields one set of solutions.[2] Believing they are greedy, selfish, and prone to violence yields another. I often give students three questions:

1. What kind of world do you want to live in?
2. How will you make that possible?
3. How would you complete the following: "Human beings are inherently _____."

Solutions also vary depending on whether one thinks individuals should change their behavior; or governments should take charge. How can we change people's behavior regarding climate change when most people do not see it as a high priority? Projections show demand for energy continuing to increase as people plug more electronic appliances into the wall, as the world's population grows, and more and more people want to live like us.[3]

The perils of the growth of capitalism and industry have been noted before with the understanding that if something is to change, it must be our culture. Since the beginning of the Industrial Revolution there are those who have seen industrialization and its effects as destructive. Charles Dickens (1812–70) captured in his many novels the lives of those destroyed by emerging industrialization. The revolutionary writers, Karl Marx (1818–83) and Frederick Engels (1844–95), described the plight of working men and women whose lives, backs, and health were being broken by laboring in the mines, mills, and factories of the 19th century. Thomas Jefferson (1743–1826) was strongly against the building of factories in America. Most of the writers of the Romantic period—Emerson, Thoreau, Melville—in the United States (c.1830–60) felt that industrialization was soul- and nature-destroying. Many Americans still write from this perspective. Virtually all advanced industrial societies have witnessed back-to-nature movements at some time in their development, as well as utopists calling for retreat from the world around them. While we may not want to go this far, how could anybody offer a rationale argument for using oil and energy to make snow and keep it frozen inside of a glass dome so that people can ski in Dubai? John Urry (2010: 207)

---

2 Jeremy Rifkin (2009: 7–9) discusses the idea that for 17 hundred years in the West we were lead to believe that humans were sinners in a fallen world, which lead to Hobbes' 19th century view that we needed the tight reign of government to keep us all from killing one another. This has now given way to what Rifkin refers to as the Enlightenment view of empathy; we do take into account the welfare of our fellow human beings.

3 The *McKinsey Quarterly* (2010), an international energy consulting firm, predicts that 80 percent of growth in the world's energy demand will come from developing nations, with China accounting for 32 percent of the growth and the Middle East for 10 percent.

has thought about the kind of scenarios we are likely to face in the future. One we are already seeing is increased tribalism and the rise of warlords who control weaponry, mobility, and access to food in areas where central governments are weakened.

Many writers on the topic of capitalism take a dim view of human nature, especially as it has been nurtured in the United States. Derrick Jensen, the author of several notable books about our planet believes we are holding the gun of an extractive culture against our heads, about to commit suicide with it. Nothing else we do will matter to future generations if we do not "stop this culture from killing the planet" (2009: 19). He lays out his ideas in a series of premises including: 1) industrial civilization is based on hierarchy and violence; 2) it is not redeemable; 3) the needs of the natural world are more important than ours; 4) the culture as a whole and most of its members are insane; 5), and, therefore, we need to resist such a culture. He reasons we must hate nature, our bodies, and ourselves. "If we did not hate the world, we could not allow it to be destroyed before our eyes. If we did not hate ourselves, we could not allow our homes—and our bodies—to be poisoned" (Jensen 2006: ix–xii). Whether or not we agree with this, we must recognize that many people are trying to figure out how to "drop out" of our existing culture to live lives that are less destructive emotionally and environmentally. And the effects of industry and capitalism's insatiable need for expansion suggest that the culture of the developed nations likely will need to change.

Movements of Opposition

If the cost of gasoline tripled, the price of a loaf of bread or a quart of milk could increase dramatically. This could *spur the growth of local economies based on barter and trade.* The local baker, farmer, and dairy producer could compete with large corporations and our food system would be more secure. Local economies in which the wealth stays in the community, rather than disappearing into an international system, would be more robust. Michael Shuman (2006) and Bill McKibben (2007) highlight the importance of supporting local economies and keeping money and resources in the community by eating, shopping, buying insurance, and banking locally, as well as creating local currencies. This is how humans did business for millennia.

On a river trip down the San Juan River from Bluff, Utah I caught up with a group of students completing the last two weeks of a semester in the wilderness, living rough. One student, who was up very early every morning and moving around because he was cold, fell into the river while trying to shoot a set of rapids and was in danger of hypothermia. Others quickly responded, giving him pieces of clothing or things they pulled out of their dry bags. As people were settling down for the night, I asked him why he had not brought more clothes to keep himself warm. His answer is still with me, "Because I want to see how little I can live on." *Lowering consumption among the industrialized nations is seen as critical to solving the problem of global warming.*

Living on little best describes the **Transition Towns Movement**, which originated in the United Kingdom and has grown in small communities in Ireland and the United States. The movement was started by Rob Hopkins, a British teacher of environmental design. It differs from most environmental movements in that it does not assume that industrial society will survive if we change our behavior just enough to avoid catastrophe. The Transition Towns Movement assumes collapse is inevitable and that we must build redundant political, social, and economic systems at the local level that will provide for basic human needs (Mooallem 2008), and prepare ourselves to live in self-sustaining communities, disconnected from the larger geopolitical world (Dumanowski 2009). A chapter was created in Ashland, Oregon in 2008 and brought together groups from the local wellness center, Gaia University, the Thriveability Institute and the Peace House. At their meetings they proposed more flexible zoning favorable to community gardens and a local currency called "Will's Bills," a reference to Ashland's being home to one of the best-known Shakespearean festivals in North America (Banner 2008). In such movements, great hope is placed in people's goodwill, their ability to build community, and their creative ability to solve problems.

Yet, as one resident of Sand Point said when asked about the Transition Towns Movement, "I like my dishwasher" (Mooallem 2008). Many people think living simply or with less is not for them. But what if people *had* to pay the *real* costs of what they consume?

Putting a Price on Carbon Emissions

The **theory of moral hazards** suggests that our behaviors are governed by what people know to be the costs of their behavior. These costs can be moral or economic. Although the need to reduce the carbon in the atmosphere is clear, the means to do so is subject to considerable debate. In a **cap-and-trade system**, such as the one the U.S. Congress has discussed, a decision would be reached about how much CO_2 could be released in any given year. Major emitters such as utility companies and manufacturing facilities would be given, or would buy at auction, permits adding up to the agreed amount. Permit holders would have a right to "pollute." As air monitoring equipment is already in place on coal-fired power plants and other energy providers that use fossil fuels, it would be relatively easy to determine whether a company was exceeding its allocation (permit). Under a cap-and-trade system the government would create a commodity worth at least $100 billion that could be sold and traded. Over time the amount of CO_2 permitted would be reduced, and the cost of releasing CO_2 would continually rise. Therefore emitters would have an incentive to develop technologies that would decrease CO_2 and costs of pollution.[4]

Under a carbon tax system consumers would pay directly for the carbon embedded in the products they buy. Behavioral economists often argue for this approach because of the direct link between behavior and costs. If I pay $11 for a gallon of gasoline, I have a strong incentive to buy a more fuel-efficient car and drive less. One problem with a carbon tax is it is not tied to a fixed target for GHG reduction, but some favor it because it is simple. Some have suggested that it would work even better if this tax were returned to tax payers on a per capita basis in the same way Alaska returns to each resident a percentage of revenues from oil extracted in the state. If everyone got the same amount of money back, those who drove fuel-efficient cars and used less energy would benefit more than those who drive large SUVs (Weisbach, et al. 2008).

But a carbon tax would differentially impact the poor in both advanced and developing countries, because the poor pay a higher percentage of their income for necessities such as energy, and high carbon taxes could mean people went without heat or fuel for cooking. This is one reason why international conferences such as Copenhagen have advanced cap-and-trade proposals. Under a global cap-and-trade system, developing nations would be given permits to emit a percentage of the world's GHGs. This would be politically easier than transferring billions of dollars from northern to southern countries, but difficult to monitor because most developing nations do not have monitoring systems in place. In short, there are no easy answers, but most policy makers and economists agree we need a market-based system. The economist, Paul Krugman (2010a: 38), has said, "[T]he very scale and complexity of the situation requires a market-based solution." Getting people to change complex behaviors is, as we learned, close to impossible, unless—in the case of climate change—we "put a price on emissions so that this cost in turn gets incorporated into everything in a way that reflects ultimate environmental impacts."

Valuing the Future

The figures for the cost of doing nothing vary greatly. One study suggests the costs will be at least $20 trillion by 2100. That is, the combined social, economic, and environmental costs of inaction will have totaled $20 trillion by 2100. Another study suggests the costs will be closer to $73 trillion by 2100. An economic model that tries to

---

4 Such a system worked for sulfur emissions from coal-fired power plants which were causing acid rain, because it allowed cuts to occur where they were cheapest. It also required action by only one government (the U.S.) and it required elaborate measuring and monitoring. It had little direct effect on consumers in terms of increased costs for energy.

predict the consequences of climate change if we do nothing to limit emissions must take into account the cost of such things as more droughts, storms, and agricultural and forestry losses, as well as savings from increasing energy efficiencies. The costs of inaction will be high. Some organizations understand this and are preparing to minimize future loss. Insurance companies that have customarily insured homes against storm damage are either sharply raising the prices of insurance or simply canceling policies. The company Swiss Re estimated that the losses from hurricane Katrina were as high as $135 billion (Galbraith 2006). The total losses (environmental, economic, and social) in the Gulf of Mexico due to the BP oil spill in 2010 could top that.

We can calculate future costs in several ways. One way would be to focus on the costs of doing nothing. Under a "business-as-usual scenario," we may have temperature increases of as high as 7–9°F over pre-industrial levels, which would have devastating and costly economic and political consequences in the near future and certainly within coming decades. We have already enumerated many of these, e.g., high-energy costs, mass migrations, political conflict, failed states, water and food shortages. A second way to think about costs is whether or not we think future generations can solve the environmental problems we have created and whether or not they will be better off than we are. In other words, should we sacrifice our current well-being for that of future generations or for our children and grandchildren? As Broome (2008) has pointed out, the value you place on your well-being, as opposed to that of future generation, is determined by ethics but can be informed by economics.

The debates about the welfare of future generations have been framed best by William Nordhaus (2007) and Nicholas Stern (2006). Sir Nicholas Stern was appointed by Tony Blair, then leader of Britain's Labor Government, to assess the consequences of what it would mean if the developed world did not take strong action to limit climate change. Blair (2006), who led the United Kingdom's determined efforts to get the nation to reduce their GHGs, said of the *Stern Review*, "It is not in doubt that if the science is right, the consequences for our planet are literally disastrous." The *Stern Review* estimated that inaction could result in the loss of up to 5 percent of the world's GDP every year, forever. And if a wider range of risks and impacts (beyond those used in the model) exist, yearly GDP loss could be 20 percent or more. The report claimed that "Our actions now and over the coming decades could create risks ... on a scale similar to those associated with the great wars and the economic depression of the first half of the 20th century" (Stern 2006: xv.) Nordhaus described the *Stern Review* as a political document with flawed economics but agreed it is important to balance economic and environmental policies. He also, like many economists, believes that carbon prices should actually reflect the social costs of greenhouse gas emissions, so that the everyday decisions of billions of firms and people can be made with knowledge about the consequences of their behavior.

The major difference between Stern's assessment and Nordhaus's revolves around something called the **discount rate**. The discount rate is extremely important. It consists of two concepts: 1) the anticipated rate of return on capital over extended periods of time, which Nordhaus calculates to be about 6 percent and Stern assumes to be a much lower rate of 1.4 percent; and, 2) the relative weight of the economic welfare of different households over a specific period of time. Both Stern and Nordhaus assume the value of goods received in the future will be less than they are today. Thus, in using a discount rate of 6 percent, as Nordhaus does, $1 trillion today will be worth only $2.5 billion in 100 years. Using Stern's discount rate of 1.4 percent the $1 trillion spent today is worth $247 billion in 100 years. Nordhaus and Stern therefore arrive at different conclusions about what we should do. Nordhaus thinks that investing 1 percent of the world's GDP ($500 billion) every year is not prudent because it will be worth far less in the future; and future generations will be richer than today's and therefore in a better position to pay for solutions to climate change. Stern comes to the opposite conclusion and argues that we must act now out of concern for future generations. If you believe that the economy can continue to grow as it has in the past, and that somehow we will be able to figure out how to mitigate and adapt to climate change in the future, then you would arrive at the same conclusion as Nordhaus. But, as I have argued in Chapters I and II, the idea of constant growth is neither sustainable nor logical. It is not sustainable because we are running out of scarce and non-renewal resources, and it is not logical because all systems have finite limits. As our society becomes more and more complex, the rate of return on our investment continues to drop. We operate with the assumption that short-term benefits outweigh long-term ones. This is one reason why it is difficult to develop strong political and economic policies that will benefit future generations, not to speak of those who are currently trapped in abysmal poverty. It also raises questions about who should pay for climate change.

Who Should Pay?

Climate change might be, as the *Economist* (2009: 4) has claimed, the hardest political problem the world has ever had to solve. It requires an immediate lowering of emissions, and a rationing of reductions among the countries of the world. Shifting to a low-carbon economy would also require businesses to change their investment patterns. When two hundred nations came to Copenhagen in December 2009 to negotiate an international climate accord, they were not of one mind about what needed to be done or even what the consequences of an agreement to lower emissions would be. Not surprisingly, some argued that a climate "deal" would wreck the U.S. economy (Lieberman 2009). China and the United States were at odds with one another about cutting emissions. China did not want a hard target that would limit its continued economic growth nor did it want its emissions monitored by others. Instead, China wanted its targets based on overall improvements in energy efficiencies.

The need to develop sustainable technologies in both the developed and developing world is imperative but it will be costly. The International Energy Agency has estimated that it will cost all nations no less than *$1 trillion a year* to hold GHGs to manageable levels (2°C). The World Bank believes investments could have the greatest impact if we focused on the still developing countries, providing them with $475 billion a year (*Economist* 2009: 20) to eliminate GHGs. The United States and other wealthy countries did agreed in Copenhagen to commit $30 billion in emergency aid over the next three years (2010–13) and by 2020, $100 billion a year to help poor nations adjust to the need to lower emissions. Lumumba Di-Aping (2009), the Sudanese ambassador who chaired the bloc of developing countries at the conference, said the agreement was disappointing and overall was a gross violation of the rights of the poor. The offer of aid was accepted, but regarded as unfair because developing countries were being asked to lower their GHGs to help solve a problem they did not cause. Earlier a spokesman for China's Foreign Ministry, Jiang Yu (2007), said developed countries' long-term emissions had caused climate change and these countries could not shirk their responsibility. Expecting a still developing nation with rich natural resources—such as potassium, bauxite, lithium, iron, oil, coal, or forests—not to use these resources to industrialize and raise their citizens out of poverty seemed a gross injustice. The argument of less developed and poor nations was that those who caused high concentrations of GHGs and who benefited from them should pay to help them limit their GHGs and to transfer money and "green" technologies to make that possible. Such an arrangement would mean that most northern countries would be required to pay into an international fund. A country like Poland, however, whose pollution was imposed on it by an external political regime intent on exploiting the environment, would not be required to pay (Heilprin 2009). The conservative columnist, Charles Krauthammer (2009), described the poor asking the rich for help as a "shakedown." We should not, he said, redistribute money from hard-working tax-paying citizens of democracies to "Third World kleptocracies." The Copenhagen climate conference ended with a non-binding agreement—the Copenhagen Accord—to lower emissions to fight climate change. Fifty nations, each of which set its own goals and timelines, signed the Copenhagen Accord. Those 50 nations account for 80 percent of the entire world's GHGs. Rapidly growing countries such as China promised to limit emissions as a percentage of their growing economy, while countries such as the United States and the United Kingdom agreed to lower their emissions from historic highs.

Copenhagen disappointed many. By the time of the Summit, several climate scientists, including James Hansen of NASA, had concluded that the original upper limit of 450 ppm was too high and, if civilization as we know it was to survive, we needed to aim for a lower limit, 350 ppm. It had been assumed that with emissions growing by about 2–3 percent a year, or 2 ppm, if humanity made Herculean efforts to reduce emissions, we could by 2050 limit the impacts of climate change. Over 450 ppm would tip the planet into chaos. (We passed the 350 mark two decades ago and are approaching 390 ppm.) To help drive the talks at Copenhagen and to call the public's attention to just how serious the problem is, Bill McKibben founded the **350 Movement**, and called for a day of worldwide demonstrations on October 24, 2009 (McKibben 2010). The idea was to help people answer the question: How much more carbon can we safely add to the atmosphere? The answer is *none* (Revkin 2009). But framing a problem as insolvable is not necessarily the best way to approach it.

Approaching the Problems: Population, Poverty, and Energy Costs

Mitigation is the reduction of GHGs in the atmosphere. **Adaptation** is the adjustment to the fact that the Earth will continue to warm because of the GHGs already in the atmosphere, as well as those GHGs we are likely to add in the future. Mitigation involves using less energy that releases CO_2. Adaptation could involve building sea walls against rising tides, or developing drought resistant crops. Most climate change writers believe a combination of approaches is essential. Earlier in this chapter we identified four tightly related problems that *must* be solved: population growth, increasing emissions, degradation of Earth's ecosystems, and poverty.

Population Growth

Population growth can cancel out *everything* we do to limit the build-up of GHGs (Attenborough 2009), and population continues to increase at a rapid rate. In 1804, the world's total population stood at about one billion people, having taken at least a million years to reach that level. But it took only 118 years for it to double to two billion in 1922. The next billion were added in only 37 years (1959) and it will take only 15 years to go from our present level of around seven billion people to eight billion in 2028. Growth has slowed slightly but it is estimated that we will reach the level of 9.2 billion by 2050 (United States Bureau of the Census 2010). The two main reasons for the rise in CO_2 emissions are the rise in population and the rise in energy use per person. If the population grows to 9.2 billion from our current level, it would be the equivalent of adding two Americas, more than two Chinas, 10 Indias, or 20 United Kingdoms. (To see population as it grows, and where it is growing, go to www.optimumpopulation.org.) Because population has been an almost taboo subject (for religious, ideological, and political reasons), governments have focused their attention on technical and economic solutions (taxes, subsidies for new technologies, etc.) to limit the impacts of climate change. Some governments even see growing populations as a good thing, because it leads to more consumers and economic growth, and is therefore a way to pay for entitlements such as Medicare and Social Security. If external costs, such as climate change and environmental degradation, are not accounted for it makes sense for governments to encourage population growth. A closer look at where populations are actually increasing is important. Earth's population was growing at a rate of 2 percent in the 1960s; it is now about 1 percent, and well below the replacement rate in Japan, Russian, and several northern European countries. But population growth well above replacement levels is concentrated in the poor countries of the world, which is where the majority of people will live by 2030. Poor people, especially in rural communities, have more children because children can help with herding and gathering food; they can also help take care of the elderly and younger children. Thus, if you do not know whether your children will live to be adults, you are likely to have more of them.

Poverty

The gap between rich and poor countries continues to grow (Central Intelligence Agency 2010); dealing with the poverty that causes high birth rates is essential. What will convince people in poor countries to have fewer children? They must know they can enjoy a decent lifestyle; there must be a predictable and substantial source of funding to create low-carbon economies and to deal with problems of water, drought, infrastructure, and education. *Education for women and universal voting rights are consistently related to declining birth rates.* There are, then, related problems that must be solved for poor countries: population growth; the need to help them generate income to allow them to participate in the 21st century; and the need to find ways to address their emerging energy needs.

As the Erlichs, who have written extensively on problems of population growth, note:

> The environmental deterioration resulting from ever more people consuming ever more resources will place the heaviest burdens on those least able to cope, as the great majority of those additional billions of people will be in the poorest nations, where poverty and high birth rates are inextricably linked.
>
> (Erlich and Erlich 2009: 36–37)

Fred Pearce (2009: 40) has argued that focusing on expanding population panders to a dangerous delusion and distracts from the real issue. "The real issue," he says, "is not overpopulation but overconsumption—mostly in rich countries that have long given up adding substantial numbers to their population." Citing the Princeton Environmental Institute, he offers a startling figure: *7 percent of the world's population—about 500,000 million people—produce 50 percent of the world's carbon emissions, while the poorest 50 percent of the population produce only 7 percent of the emissions.* These figures are one of the reasons that the poor Southern nations argued for help from Northern nations in Copenhagen.

The High Cost of Energy

We have already noted that all projections indicate that the energy needs of both the developed and developing world are going to change substantially in the next two decades. Paul Krugman (2010a) has put the challenge clearly. Because the world's population is going to grow to roughly 9.2 billion by 2050, and because "more and more of those 9.2 billion will aspire to, and be able to, live like Americans—with American-sized cars, homes, and Big Macs—demand for fossil fuels is going to go through the roof." Some days the smog and dust over Los Angeles come not from people living in Los Angeles but from Northern China, which is exporting not just consumer goods but also sulfur dioxide and soot. China relies on coal for 80 percent of its electricity, which has brought better living to many Chinese so that now 84 out of 100 urban households have air conditioners and those living in small towns and rural villages have electric stoves and refrigerators. To meet the needs of its citizens, China has been building close to one new coal-fired power plant every month for the past five years. Some, but not all, are more efficient, which means they can reduce the amount of CO_2 but not eliminate it (Bradsher, 2009; Bradsher and Barboza 2006). Coal is *not* a clean technology and some have argued that if we are to stop climate change in its tracks we must stop burning coal (Allen 2009), and many Western ranchers, farmers, and environmentalists have joined the chorus because the mining and burning of coal are destructive to their way of life (Moran 2007). But coal is cheap and people want cheap power.

There are a number of ideas for removing the CO_2 produced by coal. Some draw the CO_2 off and use it to provide industrial-grade carbon dioxide for beverages; other technologies capture CO_2 by growing algae and using the algae for fuel. A study by faculty at the Massachusetts Institute of Technology (2007) recognizes that coal is here to stay but argues that we must use new technologies, such as carbon sequestration, to reduce significantly CO_2 emissions. No new plants should be built without a means of capturing CO_2. Their solution requires additional research and government support to find ways of pumping CO_2 deep underground. No means has yet been developed to do this successfully on a large scale, although the Calera corporation (Biello 2008) has been able to capture CO_2 and use it to produce cement. Every ton of cement can capture a half ton of CO_2. This technology could reduce the price of cement to zero, if there is a market for sequestering carbon, e.g., $30+ a ton.

The problem is not that chemical, petroleum, and mining companies cannot find ways to limit the impact of carbon-based fuels; it is that it is costly to do so (Holmes 2009). Consumers are not "ready," yet, for the shock of much higher prices. Nevertheless, the reality is that we need alternatives to coal and oil, because both will become increasingly expensive and because expensive energy means that those now locked in poverty will remain there. To solve the problem of climate change and global inequities we need *less* expensive energy. It is useful to remind ourselves of why we cannot continue to rely on oil.

- It is too valuable a resource to waste by putting it in the tanks of our cars. It is used in a variety of other ways that benefit us—plastics and medications.
- It is a national security problem. Around 70 percent of all the oil in the world is owned by national oil companies in other nations: Russia, Iraq, Iran, Saudi Arabia, Venezuela.
- There is not enough of it to go around, with increasing energy needs and population growth.

The Optimists and the Pessimists

Jesse Ausubel (2009), a senior research associate at Rockefeller University in New York, believes that humans are creative and capable and that we will find a way out of our current set of circumstances. We can feed 10 billion people, *even if* we go on eating meat. All we need to do is keep improving agricultural yields by 2 percent, because population is only growing at 1 percent. We will have more forests to sequester carbon, because we'll be reading newspapers and magazines online. Our needs will drive innovation.

This line of reasoning has been referred to as "the Parable of Horseshit" (Kolbert 2009). In the 1800s, New Yorkers used horses to move goods and themselves around. By 1880 there were at least 150 thousand horses in New York, each one depositing on average 22 lb of manure a day or 45 thousand tons a month. Farmers and gardeners were at first eager to take this rich source of fertilizer but soon the supply exceeded the demand. The market was glutted; manure piled up; flies were attracted and public conversation revolved around what to do with the manure. By the early 1900s the problem no longer existed. By 1912 cars outnumbered the horses. The last horse-drawn streetcar made its final run in 1917. Technology had solved that problem.

Some put great faith in technology. Hunter and Amory Lovins (Lovins 1977, see also Hawken, Lovins, and Lovins 2008), who founded the Rocky Mountain Institute in 1982, have been strong advocates for what they call a "soft" path of solar and renewable energies, as opposed to the "hard" path of nuclear energy and fossil fuels. Along with Paul Hawken, they have argued that we can meet many of our current needs simply through the use of existing technologies and making more efficient use of fuels (Hawken, Lovins, and Lovins 2008). We could, as many have, build homes that draw almost no power from the grid because they use solar panels, geothermal pumps, or are so well-insulated that they use virtually no energy. If we are driving a car that gets 20 mpg; we could increase efficiency 50 percent by simply buying one that gets 30 mpg. We could, if we had the will to do so, solve our problems of oil dependence and climate change.

Stephen Pacala and Robert Socolow (2004), Princeton professors who lead the Carbon Mitigation Initiative, have developed a game or strategy for reducing carbon emissions over the next 50 years. They identify 15 separate strategies, or **stabilization wedges**, each one of which, they claim, could reduce global carbon emissions by one billion tons per year. The goal of the **wedge game**, used in many high school science classes across the country, is to use seven wedges from the different strategies to stabilize the climate. The four basic categories and strategies are as follows:

1. **Efficiency and conservation:** increased transportation efficiency; reduced number of miles traveled; increased heating efficiency; increased efficiency of electricity production.
2. **Fossil-fuel-based strategies:** switch from coal to natural gas; capture and storage of CO_2; use synthetic fuels derived from coal along with carbon sequestration; use of hydrogen fuels.
3. **Nuclear energy:** nuclear electricity.
4. **Renewables and biostorage:** wind, solar, and hydrogen fuel generated from wind, biofuels, forest sequestration, and soil storage (grasses).

These are all good ideas and many of them are workable. We could, for example, reduce the number of miles people travel in their cars by locating work, education, worship, shopping, and recreation within smaller communities, eliminating sprawl. Others, such as the use of hydrogen fuels to power cars, are more difficult to scale. Marty Hoffert (2005) has suggested that although all of the technologies suggested by the wedge game are available, they are not operational, and would require mass mobilization to make them so. "[H]umanity had the know-how to build nuclear weapons in the late 30s or go to the Moon in the 50s. But it took the Manhattan and Apollo programs to make it so."

Thomas Friedman (2007) has posed the problem like this. We have the technology to create solar farms, wind farms, and other forms of emission-free energy. We need to scale up all of those systems and connect them to a new electrical grid, all of which costs money. Money was no object when it came to getting to the Moon. But, he notes, asking people to pay for expensive energy, when cheap coal and oil are available, is like asking NASA to build a spaceship to the Moon, when Southwest Airlines is already flying there and you can get free peanuts too.

What Needs to Change for Action to Occur?

As I said above, Wallace put on the wrong pair of trousers and as a result ended up in places he never intended. The authors of *The Hartwell Paper* (Prins, et al. 2010) believe that those who assembled in Copenhagen in December of 2009 were all wearing the wrong pants and framing the problem in such a way that it could not be solved. Getting close to 200 nations to try and agree on their CO_2 emissions over the next decade was ineffective. Prins, et al. came up with a new set of strategies based on six principles. The developed nations of the world must:

- Ensure the basic energy needs of the world's growing populations, which means we must diversify energy sources.
- Provide energy that is inexpensive, i.e., priced below coal.
- Deal with problems of global inequality.
- Ensure economic growth and development in a way that does not threaten Earth systems, which means we must have strategies to reduce CO_2 on a systematic basis.
- Prepare to adapt to the risks and dangers of climate change, which means we need to embrace the strategies of both mitigation and adaptation.
- Remember climate is a "wicked" problem, part of a larger complex of problems like population growth, wealth disparities, technology, and resource use.

(Prins, et al. 2010: 16)

The public can better understand the need to focus on the specific things we can actually do something about, rather than the abstract notion of climate change. Solutions need to be politically attractive, with clear, rapid, and measurable paybacks. We need to value short-term gains as well as long-term gains.

It is estimated that deforestation accounts for 20 percent of all CO_2 emissions (King 2010). Forests are cut down because people want to raise cattle for national and international markets; they are cut down because hungry urban dwellers with no work and no food for their families move into isolated areas and cut down trees to create small farms. Trees are harvested in this way throughout South America, Asia, and Africa. This is a problem that can be solved by paying people not to cut down the trees and protecting the forests and the wildlife in them.[5] Another problem that could be solved is black carbon or soot, which accounts for between 5–10 percent of GHGs, and carries significant health risks. Soot also speeds the melting of Arctic and Himalayan glaciers, as the black absorbs the Sun's heat. Almost two million people die each year from black carbon, produced primarily by diesel engines and primitive stoves burning cow dung and wood. The solution: provide filters for diesel trucks and cheap, cleaner stoves for villagers (*Economist* 2009: 22).

---

5 There are many such projects throughout the world. The good ones involve the citizens of such areas in active management and have well-developed systems in place for rewarding people for taking care of resources that benefit not only them but the entire Earth. Others benefit mainly those from developed countries, and shut native people out of preserves that have been established to protect endangered wildlife and unique bioregions. Any system that addresses deforestation will have to take into account, and pay more for, the most vulnerable systems.

We do not simply provide developing nations with more money. That has not worked; aid dollars flowing to Africa have not raised per capita income. We need to develop *targeted programs* that help to grow local and regional economies, *help women become educated,* help people to *restore ecosystems* so they can grow traditional crops, and help them *benefit from the natural resources* they have (Parker 2010). This means meeting the demand of developing nations for the transfer of green technologies.

New Technologies

I noted above that it is the cheap price of coal that serves to check the use of new technologies. As long as the Sun keeps shining, the Earth spinning, magma stays boiling, and the laws of gravity do not change, we have unlimited amounts of energy that can be captured from solar panels, wave machines, wind turbines, water turbines, and turbines driven by geothermal energy. The Sun constantly throws out 120 quadrillion watts of energy to the Earth's surface, more in one hour than we use in an entire year.

Solar Energy

Solar energy can be used in many ways. Sunlight can be concentrated by reflected mirrors to boil water to drive steam turbines, which can then make electricity or be used to make hydrogen, which can in turn be used to power a new generation of cars. Other solar arrays heat oil, which in turn is used to heat water, make steam, and drive turbines. In Spain there are massive solar fields that use the Sun to heat salt, which retains its heat into the hours of darkness, making it possible to get 7.5 more hours of energy (Johnson 2009). We all know about solar panels that can convert sunlight directly into electricity for homes and business. We could, in the United States, meet most of our energy needs by putting panels on every available roof. Even though panels are becoming much more efficient, an average kilowatt costs at least $5,000, often more, compared with coal at $1,800. Solar might save us, but it would be costly.

Wind Turbines

Wind turbines are also an effective way to generate electricity. China leads the world in wind generation with 10 gigawatts (GW) (one billion kilowatts) of power. As the average home in United States uses about 10,000 kilowatts a year, a one GW system would power 100,000 homes. The Great Plains of the United States, from North Dakota down to Oklahoma and the Panhandle of Texas, have the potential to generate as much as 300 GW of energy. The United States Department of Energy (2008) believes that this could meet 20 percent of the nation's needs by 2030. Wind turbines are clean, use no water, and produce cheap energy (3.4 cents per kilowatt), at slightly more than the price of coal (3 cents).

Nuclear Power

Nuclear power plants are expensive to build, cheap to operate, and do not pour carbon dioxide into the air. Once they are up and running they produce cheap electricity (3.3 cents). We have used small nuclear-powered systems to power our submarine fleet for years without incident. There are new fourth-generation technologies for reactors that are more efficient than the first-generation reactors and produce less of a waste stream (Wald 2009). There is less than one-in-a-million chance that an accident would happen at a nuclear plant, but not everyone wants to take those odds.

Biofuels

Right now we pour 140 billion gallons of gasoline a year into our cars; which at $3.00 per gallon is $420 billion a year spent on a non-renewable resource. Seventy percent of the oil we use each year (eight billion barrels) is used to power tractors, cars, airplanes, motorcycles, lawnmowers, and chainsaws. We have a problem to solve. We can solve it by making fuel from sources other than oil. We already make methanol from wood products; we can turn algae into oil and into ethanol and butanol and we can make ethanol from corn. We have promising technologies for using genetically engineered catalysts to break down the cellulose in woody fibers and grasses to transform that into sugars that can then be used to make fuel. Alternative fuels sound good because we already have a well-developed distribution system (gas stations) to use them. But here is the "wicked" part: we should not be using some of these sources to power our cars. Some of them, like ethanol, require more energy to produce than we get from it (Grunwald 2008). Why are we using it? Because of price subsidies for corn and subsidies for the fuel itself.

To put things in perspective, right now the United States gets 68.5 percent of its energy from fossil fuels, another 23 percent from nuclear power and other sources, and 8.5 percent from renewables such as solar, wind, hydro, geothermal, and biomass. If current trends continue without significant new investment, by 2030 the United States would still get most of its energy (65 percent) from fossil fuels and only 17 percent from renewable resources. It will take expanded research programs and government subsidies to expand the use of "green" energy (Johnson 2009: 53).

Geoengineering

If we want to avoid the most serious effects of climate change we could create artificial trees that filter CO_2 out of the air and extract it for storage. Or we could fertilize the oceans with iron. Iron would stimulate a phytoplankton bloom, which would benefit the marine food chain and also sequester carbon (Brahic 2009). There have been at least 13 international teams who have done this since 1993 and a venture-capital firm in California is trying to make this commercially viable, assuming there would be monetary benefits for sequestering carbon. We could also spray sulfur into the air (as occurs when a volcano erupts) or other aerosols that would deflect solar energy. We could place large reflecting mirrors in deserts and increase the Earth's albedo effect; we could paint the roofs of all our houses white. We could put into orbit space reflectors. One problem with these schemes is that we don't know if they would all work and we do not know what their interactive effect would be with all of Earth's systems. But they might be essential experiments to make if we cannot control our growing worldwide need for energy.

Finally, There is our Behavior

What if you ate less meat? Rajendra Pachuri, who heads the IPCC panel on climate change, has suggested one meat-free meal a week as a way for us to reduce our individual **carbon footprint**. Americans eat a lot of meat a year. In 1950, we ate 150 lb a year, in 1981 it was 238 lb, and we are now eating almost 300 lb a year. We're not alone; world meat consumption, though not as high as ours, went from 62 lb in 1981 to 88 lb in 2002. China has seen a dramatic increase jumping from 33 lb to 115 lb in the same time period (Adler 2008). Cattle, pigs, chickens, and farm-raised fish produce waste and require substantial amounts of grain and water. It takes, on average, about 12 lb of grain to get 1 lb of beef and it takes a lot of energy, in the form of petroleum-based fertilizers, to grow the grain and transport it to concentrated animal feed operations (CAFOs).

Americans use 2.5 million plastic bottles every hour and we throw 70 percent of them away. We also throw away 25 billion Styrofoam cups and make enough plastic film to shrink-wrap Texas, an intriguing thought. If we recycled just one plastic bottle we could save enough energy to power our computer for 25 minutes (NRWS 2010). So why don't we?

Why Don't We Act?

One reason for inaction is that many of us simply do not know what the impact of our behavior is. Here are three websites that are widely used to calculate our impact on the Earth. Use one of them and then consider why the average American uses as many resources as 32 Kenyans and whether or not this will allow us to achieve a sustainable future.

- http://coolclimate.berkeley.edu
- http://www.footprintnetwork.org
- http://www.epa.gov/climatechange/emissions/ind_calculator.html.

Another reason we do not act is that we do not suffer the consequences of our behavior. The real price of a gallon of gas is almost $11 a gallon. Gas priced at this level in

Europe has led to the use of smaller and lighter cars, better insulated homes, development of public transportation systems, and compact urban neighborhoods.

Taxing carbon and requiring us to pay for our environmental, economic, and social impacts will require significant political will, which is one of the reasons it has not yet happened. We can grow a "green" economy in which renewable energy and "green" jobs become our future (Daly 1996). We need to work on both mitigation and adaptation, as noted above. So far, most of the national and international discussions have revolved around mitigation, lessening the amount of carbon dioxide in the air through the use of new "green" technologies. The proper role for a government in helping to develop such systems is to set consistent price signals, so that those willing to invest in new "green" technologies know there is a market. Subsidies, or tax breaks, are a public policy issue, which you help to shape. It is your tax dollars that will determine which investments we make. Without consistent price signals there is extreme volatility in the markets. For a free-market system to work, then, government needs to play a role in helping to create markets for "green" products. It also needs to assure that companies do not "cheat" by externalizing costs in third-world countries or even our own.

It is essential that we focus our energies on problems we can solve. It is essential that we all recognize that:

- Climate change is real.
- Humans are contributing to the warming of the planet.
- Science supports these findings.
- We have a difficult time understanding the consequences of our actions.
- There are solutions to the problems we face.
- Climate change cannot be solved in isolation from other related problems such as population growth, high-energy costs, and global inequalities.
- Focus your own energy where it can make the greatest difference.

DISCUSSION QUESTIONS

1. Explain how the concept of the tragedy of the commons is relevant to understanding climate change. What are things that we share in common and who is responsible for assuring the sustainability of those resources?
2. Can the problem of climate change be solved without solving such problems as population growth or global inequality? Explain why.
3. Using the theory of moral hazards, outline those policies that should be created to get people to change their behavior and reduce their greenhouse gas emissions.
4. Why do some argue that the United States needs to provide global leadership and financial support to reduce greenhouse gas emissions?
5. What are the things that everyone should know about climate change? How would you convince others that climate change is real and that action is required?

Bibliography

Adam, David. 2009. "ExxonMobil Continuing to Fund Climate Skeptic Groups, Records Show." *Guardian* (July 1).

Adler, Ben. 2008. "Are Cows Worse than Cars?" *The American Prospect* (December 3). Retrieved October 26, 2010 (http: //www.prospect.org).

Allen, Myles. 2005. "A Novel View of Global Warming: Review of *State of Fear*." *Nature 433*: 198.

———. 2009. "Leave that Coal Alone." Cited in *New Scientist* (May 2): 4.

Americanpolicy.org. May 2, 2007. "There is no Global Warming." Retrieved December 4, 2010.

Anderegg, William, R. L., James W. Prall, Jacob Harold, and Stephen H. Schneider. 2010. "Expert Credibility in Climate Change." *Proceedings of the National Academy of Sciences 86*(1073): 1–3.

Archer, David, Bruce Buffet, and Victor Brovkin. 2009. "Ocean Methane Hydrates as a Slow Tipping Point in the Global Carbon Cycle." *Proceedings of the National Academy of Sciences 106*(49): 96–101.

Associated Press. 2006. "Bush Gives Thumbs Down to Gore's New Movie." Retrieved June 24, 2010 (http://www.msnbc.msn.com/id/12930351).

———. 2009. "EPA View Gets Chilly Reaction." (December 8).

Attenborough, David. 2009. "The Crowded Planet": Interview with David Attenborough by Alison George. *New Scientist* (May 16): 28–29.

Ausubel, Jesse. 2009. "Ingenuity Wins Every Time." Interview by Alison George. *New Scientist* (September 26): 38–39.

Baldassare, Mark, Dean Bonner, Jennifer Paluch, and Sonja Petek. 2009. *Californians and the Environment*. San Francisco: Public Policy Institute of California (July): 1–34.

Ballantyne, Ashely, D. R. Greenwood, J. S. Sinninghe Damasté, A. Z. Csank, and N. Rbyczynski. 2010. "Significantly Warming Arctic Surface Temperatures during the Pliocene Indicated by Multiple Independent Proxies." *Geology 38*: 603–06.

Banner, Bob. 2008. "Transition Town Movement Comes to Ashland." Accessed online at http://www.transitionalcalifornia.ning.com/profiles/blogs/transition-town-movement-comes.

Barringer, Felicity. 2008. "Personal Communication at California State University, Chico," for the annual *This Way to Sustainability* conference. November 5.

Bernstein, Peter. 1996. *Against the Gods: The Remarkable Story of Risk*. New York: John Wiley.

Berry, Wendell. 2008. "Faustian Economics: Hell Hath No Limits." *Harper's Magazine* (May). Retrieved July 20, 2010 (http://www.harpers.org/archive/2008).

Biello, David. 2008. "Cement from CO_2: A Concrete Cure for Global Warming?" *Scientific American* (August 7). Accessed online at http: //www.scientificamerican.com.

Black, Richard. 2009. "E-mail Row to Affect Copenhagen." *BBC News.* Retrieved June 15, 2010 (http://bbc.co.uk/go/pr/-2/science/nature/8392611.stm).

Blair, Tony. 2006. "PM's Comments at Launch of Stern Review." (October 30). Retrieved June 15, 2010 (http://www.number-10.gov.uk/output/Page10300.asp).

Borenstein, Seth. 2006. "Scientists OK Gore's Movie for Accuracy." *Washington Post* (June 27).

Boykoff, Maxwell, and Jules Boykoff. 2004. "Balance as Bias: Global Warming and the U.S. Prestige Press." *Global and Environmental Change 14*: 1.

Bradsher, Keith. 2009. "China Outpaces U.S. in Cleaner Coal-Fired Plants." *New York Times* (May 10). Retrieved October 26, 2010 (http: //www.nytimes.com/2009/05/11...11coal.html).

Bradsher, Keith, and David Barboza. 2006. "Pollution from Chinese Coal Casts a Global Shadow." *New York Times* (June 11). Retrieved October 26, 2010 (http: //www.nytimes.com/2006...11-chinacoal.html).

Brahic, Catherine. 2009. "If Emissions Cuts Are Not Enough." *New Scientist* (September 5): 10.

Brennan, Phillip V. 2009. "Global Cooling Headed Our Way." Retrieved October 26, 2010 (http://www.newsmax.com/brennen/ice_age_cooling/2009/01/13/170804.html).

British Antarctic Survey. 2007. "BAS Statement about Channel 4 Programme on Global Warming." Retrieved June 22, 2010 (http://www.antarctic.uk).

Broome, John. 2008. "The Ethics of Climate Change." *Scientific American* (June): 97–102.

Brown, Lester. 2009. *Plan B 4.0: Mobilizing to Save Civilization.* New York: Norton.

Brundtland, Gro H. (ed.) 1987. *Our Common Future.* Oxford, United Kingdom: Oxford University Press. Retrieved October 26, 2010 (http://www.worldinbalance.net/intagreements/1987-brundtland.php).

Central Intelligence Agency. 2010. "Oil Consumption by Country." Retrieved October 26, 2010 (http://www.cia.gov).

Chaudhaury, Rajendra. 2009. Reported in the *New Scientist* (July 18): 8.

Clarke, Lee. 2010. "The Nuclear Option." Pp. 308–16 in *Routledge Handbook of Climate Change*, ed. Constance Tracy-Lever. London and New York: Routledge.

Cole, K. C. 1998. *The Universe and the Teacup: The Mathematics of Truth and Beauty.* New York: Harcourt.

Cook, David. 2010. "Carbon Dioxide in the Atmosphere." Argonne National Laboratory. Retrieved July 2, 2010 (http://www.anl.gov).

Crichton, Michael. 2004. *State of Fear.* New York: Harper Collins.

Daly, Herman. 1996. *Beyond Growth: The Economics of Sustainable Development.* Boston: Beacon Press.

Diamond, Jared. 2005. *Collapse: How Societies Choose to Fail or Succeed.* New York: Viking Press.

Di-Aping, Lumumba. 2009. Cited in Arthur Max, "Climate Deal Elicits Little Enthusiasm." *Sacramento Bee* (December 19). Associated Press Report.

Diffenbaugh, Noah S., Moetasim Ashfaq, Ying Shi, Wen-wen Tung, Robert J. Trapp, Jueijie Gao, and Jeremy Pal. 2009. "Suppression of South Asian Summer Monsoon Precipitation in the 21st Century." *Geophysical Research Letters: American and Geophysical Union 36*: 1–5.

Dumanowski, Dianne. 2009. *The End of the Long Summer*. New York: Random House.

Dunlap, Riley, and Aaron McCright. 2008. "A Widening Gap: Republican and Democratic Views on Climate Change." *Environment Magazine 50*(5): 26–34.

———. 2010. "Climate Change Denial: Sources, Actors, and Strategies." Pp. 240–59 in *Handbook of Climate Change and Society*, ed. Constance Lever-Tracy. London and New York: Routledge.

Economist. 2009. "Getting Warmer: A Special Report on Climate Change and the Carbon Economy." *Economist* (December 5).

Enterprise Record. 2010. "Editorial: Voters Will Have a Say on AB32." *Enterprise Record* (June 25): 6A.

Environmental Protection Agency. 2009. "Climate Change: Atmospheric Changes." Retrieved July 2, 2010 (http://www.epa.gov/climatechange/science/recentac.html).

Erlich, Paul, and Anne Erlich. 2009. "Enough of Us Now." *New Scientist* (September 26): 36–37.

Flannery, Tim. 2009. *Now or Never: Why We Must Act Now to End Climate Change and Create a Sustainable Future*. New York: Atlantic Monthly Press.

Foreign Policy. 2010. "Failed States Index." Retrieved October 26, 2010 (http://www.foreignpolicy.com).

Friedman, Thomas L. 2007. "The Power of Green." *New York Times* (April 15): 40–51, 67, 71.

Galbraith, Kate. 2006. "The Trillion Dollar Question: What's the Real Cost of Climate Change and Where Do All Those Numbers Come From?" *Grist* (November 16). Retrieved July 2, 2010 (http://www.grist.org/article/galbraith2).

Gelbspan, Ross. 2005a. *Boiling Point: How Politicians, Big Oil and Coal, Journalists, and Activists Have Fueled the Climate Crisis–and What We Can Do to Avert Disaster*. New York: Basic Books.

———. 2005b. "Snowed." *Mother Jones* (May/June): 42–43.

Giles, Jim. 2009. "Fair Footprint Means Carbon Bankruptcy." *New Scientist* (September 19): 14.

Global Issues. 2010. "Poverty Facts and Stats." Retrieved July 4, 2010 (http://www.globalissues.org/article/26/poverty-facts-and-stats).

Goodstein, Eban. 2007. *Fighting for Love in the Century of Extinction*. Burlington, Vermont: University of Vermont Press.

Gore, Al. 1992. *Earth in the Balance: Ecology and the Human Spirit*. New York: Plume.

———. 2006. *An Inconvenient Truth: The Planetary Emergency of Global Warming and What We Can Do About It*. Emmaus, PA: Rodale.

———. 2010. "We Can't Wish Away Climate Change." *New York Times* (February 28): 11.

Greenert, J. W. Admiral U.S. Navy. 2010. "Navy Climate Change Roadmap." Retrieved October 26, 2010 (http://www.navy.mil/navydata/documents/CCR.pdf).

Grist. 2006. "The CEI Ads" (May 17). Accessed online at: http://www.grist.org/article/the-cei-ads.

Grunwald, Michael. 2008. "The Clean Energy Scam." *Time* (April 7): 40–45.

Hansen, Jim. 2006. "Threat to the Planet." *New York Review of Books* (July 13). Retrieved July 1, 2010 (http://www.nybooks.com/authors/12233).

Hardin, Garrett. 1968. "Tragedy of the Commons." *Science 162* (December 13): 1243–48.

Hawken, Paul, Amory Lovins, and L. Hunter Lovins. 2008. *Natural Capitalism: Creating the Next Industrial Revolution*. Boston: Back Bay Press.

Heartland Institute. 2007. "Careful Review of Science Refutes Global Warming Myths." Jay Lehr, Science Director for the Heartland Institute. Retrieved October 24, 2010 (http://www.heartland.org/policybot/results/20645/Careful_Review_of_Science_Refutes_Global_Warming_Myths.html).

Heilprin, John. 2009. "Nations Seek Climate Financing for Poor Countries." *Associated Press* (December 11).

Heinberg, Richard. 2007. *Peak Everything: Waking Up to the Century of Declines*. Gabriola Island, British Columbia, Canada: New Society Publishers.

Hoegh-Gulberg, Ove, and John F. Bruno. 2010. "The Impact of Climate Change on Marine Ecosystems." *Science Magazine* (June 18): 1523–1528.

Hoffert, Marty. 2005. "Low-Carbon Sustainable Energy in the Greenhouse Century." Retrieved October 26, 2010 (http://www.altenergyaction.org).

Hoffmann, Matthias, and Stefan Rahmstorf. 2009. "On the Stability of the Atlantic Meridional Overturning Circulation." *Publications of the National Academy of Sciences 106*(49): 84–89.

Holdren, John. 2009. "Interview with John Holdren." *New Scientist* (August 1): 26.

Holmes, Bob. 2009. "Can Oil from Tar Sands Be Cleaned Up?" *New Scientist* (April 18): 8–19.

Houghton, John. 2007. "The Great Global Warming Swindle." Retrieved June 22, 2010 (http://www.jri.org.uk/new/Critique_Channel4_Gobal_Warming_Swindle.pdf).

Hubbert, M. King. 1976. "Exponential Growth as a Transient Phenomenon in Human History." Retrieved July 3, 2010 (http://www.hubbertpeak.com/hubbert/wwf1976).

Hulme, Mike. 2009. "The True Meaning of Climate Change." *New Scientist* (September 5): 28–29.

Inhofe, James M. 2005. "Climate Change Update: Senate Floor Statement." United States Senate. Retrieved October 26, 2010 (http://inhofe.senate.gov/pressreleases/climateupdate.htm).

Intergovernmental Panel on Climate Change (IPPC). 2007. *Climate Change 2007: The Physical Science Basis*. Cambridge: Cambridge University Press.

Jacques, Peter J., Riley E. Dunlap, and Mark Freeman. 2008. "The Organization of Denial: Conservative Think Tanks and Environmental Scepticism." *Environmental Politics 17* (June): 349–85.

Janofsky, Michael. 2006. "Bush's Chat with Novelist Alarms Environmentalists." *New York Times* (February 19).

Jensen, Derrick. 2006. *Endgame: Resistance, Volumes 1 and 2*. New York: Seven Stories Press.

———. 2009. "World at Gunpoint." *Orion* (May/June): 18–19.

Johnson, George. 2009. "Plugging into the Sun." *National Geographic* (September): 28–53.

Johnson, Tim. 2010. "Mexico Trusts its Water—if it's Bottled." *McClatchy Newspapers* (May 29).

Kahneman, Daniel, and Amos Tversky. 1979. "Prospect Theory: An Analysis of Decision Making Under Risk." *Econometrica 47*(2): 263–92.

Karlin, Anotoly. 2010. "Review of Limits to Growth." *Sublime Oblivion*. Blog. Retrieved June 29, 2010 (http://www.sublimeoblivion.com).

Kasler, Dale. 2010. "Climate Law Study Called 'Truly Weird'." *Sacramento Bee* (March 19): 1, 10.

Kimbrell, Andrew, Joseph Mendelson, Mark Briscoe, Evan Harrje, Blake Ethridge, Amy Brickner, Karmen Kallio, Jennifer Beck, and Jessica Dixon-Steeter. 1998. *The Real Price of Gasoline: An Analysis of the Hidden External Costs Consumers Pay to Fuel Their Automobiles*. Washington, DC: National Center for Technology Assessment.

King, David. 2010. "No Cause for Climate Despair." *New Scientist* (June 19): 3.

Klein, Naomi. 2010. "Gulf Oil Spill: A Hole in the World." *Guardian* (June 19). Retrieved June 19, 2010 (http://guardian.co.uk).

Kolbert, Elizabeth. 2009. "Hosed: Is There a Quick Fix for the Climate?" *New Yorker* (November 12).

Krauthammer, Charles. 2009. "The New Socialism Behind Talk about Environment." *Washington Post* (December 11).

Krugman, Paul. 2010a. "Building a Green Economy." *New York Times Magazine* (April 5). Retrieved June 25, 2010 (http://www.nytimes.com/2010/04/magazine/11Economy-t.html).

———. 2010b. "Stubborn GOP Stalls Meaningful Energy Legislation in Senate." *New York Times* (July 22).

Ladurie, Emmanuel le Roy. 1971. *Times of Feast, Times of Famine: A History of Climate Since the Year 1000.* New York: Farrar, Straus and Giroux.

Lea, Stephen. 2010. "Mind over Money." *New Scientist* (May 8): 24–25.

Leiserowitz, Anthony. 2004. "Before and after the Day after Tomorrow: A U.S. Study of Climate Change Risk Perception." *Environment 46* (November): 22–44.

Lenton, Timothy L., Herman Held, Elmar Kreigler, Jim W. Hall, Wolfgang Lucht, Stephen Rahmstorf, and Hans Joachim Schelnhuber. 2009. "Tipping Points in the Earth System." *Proceedings of the National Academy of Sciences 105*: 1786–93.

Levermann, Anders, Jaboc Schewe, Vladimir Petoukov, and Hermann Held. 2009. "Basic Mechanism for Abrupt Monsoon Transition." *Publications of the National Academy of Sciences 106*(49): 72–77.

Levitt, Steven D., and Stephen J. Dubner. 2009. *Super-Freakonomics.* New York: Harper Collins.

Lieberman, Ben. 2009. "Kyoto-like Pact Would Take Toll on Economy." *Missoulian* (November 29). McClatchy Newspapers.

Littlemore, Richard. 2010. "Manufacturing Doubt." *New Scientist* (May/June): 41.

Longfellow, Brenda. 2006. "Weather Report: Images from the Climate Crisis." Pp. 1–15 in *Coming to Terms with Nature: Socialist Register 2007*, eds. L. Panitch and C. Leys. Halifax, Nova Scotia: Fernwood Publishing.

Lovelock, James. 2006. *The Revenge of Gaia: Why the Earth is Fighting Back—and How We Can Still Save Humanity.* Santa Barbara, CA: Allen Lane.

Lovins, Amory B. 1977. *Soft Energy Paths: Toward a Durable Peace.* New York: Penguin.

Lowry, Rich. 2009. "Global Warming Believers Muzzle Voices of Dissent." *Sacramento Bee* (December 9): A19.

McCright, Aaron M., and Riley E. Dunlap. 2010. "Anti-Reflexivity: The American Conservative Movement's Success in Undermining Climate Science and Policy." *Theory, Culture & Society 27*(2–3): 100–33.

McKibben, Bill. 2007. *The Deep Economy: The Wealth of Communities and the Durable Future.* New York: Henry Holt.

———. 2010. *350.org.* Retrieved July 20, 2010 (http://www.350.org/).

McKinsey Quarterly. 2010. *World Energy Markets* (June). Accessed online at: http://www.mckinsey-quarterly.com.

McNall, Scott G. 2010. "We Have Met the Enemy and He is Us." Pp. 22–44 in *Sustainable Communities Design Handbook*, ed. Woodrow W. Clark, II. New York: Elsevier.

Mahli, Yadvinder, J. Timons Roberts, Richard A. Betts, Wenhong Li, and Carlos Nobre. 2008. "Climate Change, Deforestation and the Fate of the Amazon." *Science Magazine 319*: 169–72.

Mandia, Scott A. 2010. *Global Warming: Man and Myth.* Selden, NY: Suffolk University. Retrieved October 25, 2010 (http://www2.sunysuffolk.edu/mandias/global_warming).

Massachuetts Institute of Technology. 2007. *The Future of Coal*. Retrieved October 26, 2010 (http://web.mit.edu/coal).

Meadows, Donella, Dennis L. Meadows, Jorgen Randers, and William W. Behrens III. 1972. *The Limits to Growth*. New York: Universe Books.

Meadows, Donella, Jorgen Randers, and Dennis Meadows. 2004. *Limits to Growth: The 30-Year Update*. White River Junction, VT: Chelsea Green Publishing Company and Earthscan.

Meyerhoff, Al. 2008. "It's Getting Hot." *Sacramento Bee* (April 27): E1: 4.

Michaels, David. 2008. *Doubt is Their Product*. New York: Oxford University Press.

Mooallem, Jon. 2008. "The End is Near!" *New York Times Magazine* (April 19): 28–32, 34.

Moran, Susan. 2007. "Coal Plants' New Foes." *New York Times* (October 28).

Moser, Susan C., and Lisa Dilling. 2004. "Making Climate Hot: Communicating the Urgency and Challenge of Global Climate Change." *Environment* 46: 32–46.

National Aeronautic and Space Agency. 2010. "Roger Revelle Biography." Retrieved July 1, 2010 (http://www.earthobservatory.nasa.gov/Features/Revelle).

National Aeronautic and Space Agency, and Goddard Institute for Space Studies. 2010. "GISS Surface Temperature Analysis." Retrieved September 16, 2010 (http: //data.giss.nasa.gov/gistemp/graphs/).

National Association of Manufacturers. 2009. "Manufacturers Position on Climate Change Issues." Retrieved October 25, 2010 (http://www.nam.org/Issues/Energy-and-Climate/Manufacturing-Climate-Change.aspx).

National Intelligence Council. 2008. *Global Trends 2025: A Transformed World*. Washington, D.C.: U.S. Government Printing Office.

National Oceanic and Atmospheric Administration. 2010. "Global Warming: Frequently Asked Questions." Retrieved July 3, 2010 (http://www.ncdc.noaa.gov/oa/climate/globalwarming.html).

National Science Foundation. 2004. "Science and Technology: Public Attitudes and Understanding." Retrieved June 23, 2010 (http://www.nsf.gov/statistics/).

New Scientist. 2009. "Why There's no Sign of a Climate Conspiracy in Hacked E-Mails." Editorial. *New Scientist* (December 12): 16.

Nielsen. 2007. "Global Consumers Vote Al Gore, Oprah Winfrey and Kofi Annan Most Influential to Champion Global Warming Cause." *Nielsen Survey* (July 2). Retrieved October 26, 2010 (http://www.en-us.nielsen.com).

Nordhaus, William. 2007. "Economics: Critical Assumptions in the Stern Review on Climate Change." *Science* (July 13): 201–02.

Notz, Dirk. 2009. "The Future of Sea Ice Sheets and Sea Ice: Between Reversible Retreat and Unstoppable Loss." *Proceedings of the National Academy of Sciences 106*(49): 90–95.

NRWS (Northern Recycling and Waste Services). 2010. "NRWS News." Newletter. San Francisco, California. July/September.

Oreskes, Naomi, and Erik M. Conway. 2010. *Merchants of Doubt: How a Handful of Scientists Obscured the Truth on Issues from Tobacco Smoke to Global Warming*. New York: Bloomsbury Press.

Orr, David. 2005. *The Last Refuge: Patriotism, Politics, and the Environment in an Age of Terror*. Washington, D.C.: Island Press.

———. 2009. *Down to the Wire: Confronting Climate Collapse*. New York: Oxford University Press.

Overpeck, Jonathan, and Bradley Udall. 2010. "Climate Change: Dry Times Ahead." *Science* (June 25): 1642–43.

Pacala, Steven, and Robert Socolow. 2004. "Stabilization Wedges: Solving the Climate Problem for the Next 50 Years with Current Technologies." *Science* 305(5686): 968–72.

Parker, Ian. 2010."The Poverty Lab." *New Yorker* (May 17): 79–91.

Parsons, Christi, and Jim Tankersley. 2009. "EPA Says Climate is Health Danger." *Chicago Tribune* (December 8).

Pearce, Fred. 2007. *With Speed and Violence: Why Scientists Fear Tipping Points in Climate Change.* Boston: Beacon Press.

———. 2009. "The Greedy Few." *New Scientist* (September 26): 40.

PEW Research Center, 2009. "Economy, Jobs Top all other Policy Priorities." Retrieved September 16, 2010 (http://people-press.org/report/485/economy-top-policy-priority).

———. 2010. "Fewer Americans See Solid Evidence of Global Warming." Retrieved June 25, 2010 (http://people-press.org/report/536/global-warming).

Prins, Gwyn, Isabel Galiana, Christopher Green, Reiner Grundmann, Mike Hulme, Atte Korhola, Frank Laird, Ted Nordhaus, Roger Pielke, Jr., Steve Rayner, Daniel Sarewitz, Michael Shellenberger, Nico Stehr, and Horoyuki Tezuka. 2010. *The Hartwell Paper: A New Direction for Climate Policy after the Crash of 2009.* Oxford and London: Oxford Institute for Science, Innovation and Society, and London School of Economics (Mackinder Programme for the Study of Long Wave Events). Retrieved June 3, 2010 (http://www.lse.ac.uk/collections/mackinderProgramme/theHartwellPaper).

Prins, Gwyn, and Steve Rayner. 2007. *The Wrong Trousers: Radically Rethinking Climate Policy.* United Kingdom: Joint Discussion Paper of the James Martin Institute for Science and Civilization, University of Oxford and the MacKinder Center for the Study of Long-Wave Events, London School of Economics.

Ravilious, Kate. 2009. "Ice Age Took Hold in Less than a Year." *New Scientist* (November 14): 1.

Rayner, Steve, 2006. "Wicked Problems: Clumsy Solutions." First Jack Beale Memorial Lecture, University of New South Wales, Sydney, Australia. July 25.

Revkin, Andrew. 2009. "Campaign to Reduce Carbon Dioxide Levels Picks a Number to Make a Point." *New York Times* (October 25): 6.

Rifkin, Jeremy. 2009. *The Empathic Civilization: The Race to Global Consciousness in a World of Crisis.* New York: Penguin.

Ritter, Michael E. 2009. *The Physical Environment: An Introduction to Physical Geography.* Retrieved July 1, 2010 (http://www.uwsp.edu/geo/faculty/ritter/geog101/textbook).

Roberts, David. 2010. "Murkowski Resolution Goes Down to Defeat." *Grist.* Retrieved October 26, 2010 (http://www.grist.org/article/2010-06-10).

Robinson, Arthur B., Noah E. Robinson, and Willie Soon. 2010. "The Environmental Effects of Increased Carbon Dioxide." Cave Junction, Oregon: Oregon Institute of Science and Medicine. Retrieved October 25, 2010 (http://www.oism.org/pproject/s33p357.htm).

Rosa, Eugene A., and Thomas Deitz. 1998. "Climate Change and Society: Speculation, Construction, and Scientific Investigation." *International Sociology* 13: 425–55.

Saunders, Sam C. 1996. "Mathematics, Decision Making, and Risk Perceptions." *Mathematics Awareness Week.* Retrieved July 13, 2010 (http://www.mathaware.org/mam/96/resources/saunders.html).

Schellennhuber, Hans Joachim. 2009. "Tipping Elements in the Earth System." *Proceedings of the National Academy of Sciences 106*(49): 51–63.

Schkade, David A., and Daniel Kahneman. 1998. "Does Living in California Make People Happy? A Focusing Illusion in Judgments of Life Satisfaction." *Psychological Science 9*: 340–46.

Schumacher, Betty. 2010. "Letter to the Editor." *Enterprise Record*. Chico, California (February 27): 6A.

Shuman, Michael H. 2006. *The Small-Mart Revolution: How Local Businesses are Beating the Global Competition*. San Francisco: Berrett-Koehler.

Slovic, Paul, Melissa L. Finucare, Ellen Peters, and Donald G. MacGregor. 2004. "Risk as Analysis and Risk as Feelings: Some Thoughts about Reason, Risk, and Rationality." *Risk Analysis 24*: 1–12.

Solnit, Rebecca. 2009. *A Paradise Built in Hell: The Extraordinary Communities that Arise in Disasters*. New York: Penguin.

Solomon, Simon. 2010. *Water: The Epic Struggle for Wealth, Power, and Civilization*. New York: Harper Collins.

Soron, Dennis. 2010. "Capitalism versus Nature: Eco-Socialist Approaches to the Climate Crisis." Pp. 76–93 in *Routledge Handbook of Climate Change and Society*, ed. Constance Lever-Tracy. London and New York: Routledge.

Source Watch. 2010. "Oregon Institute of Science and Medicine." Retrieved June 24, 2010 (http://www.sourcewatch.org).

Steingraber, Sandra. 2008. "Environmental Amnesia." *Orion* (May/June). Retrieved July 17, 2010 (http://www.orionmagazine.org/index).

Stern, Nicholas. 2007. *The Economics of Climate Change: The Stern Review*. Cambridge, UK: Cambridge University Press.

Surowiecki, James. 2010. "Greater Fools." *New Yorker* (July 5): 23.

Swim, Janet, Susan Clayton, Tomas Doherty, Robert Gifford, George Howard, Joseph Reser, Paul Stern, and Elke Weber. 2009. *Psychology and Climate Change: Addressing a Multi-faced Phenomenon and Set of Challenges*. Report by the American Psychological Association's Task Force on the Interface between Psychology and Global Climate Change. Retrieved July 1, 2010 (http://www.apa.org/science/climate-change). See both the original report August 2009 and the edited report March 2010.

Szasz, Andrew. 2008. *Shopping Our Way to Safety*. Minneapolis, MN: University of Minnesota Press.

Tainter, Joseph A. 1988. *The Collapse of Complex Societies*. Cambridge, UK: Cambridge University Press.

Toynbee, Arnold. 1934–61. *The Study of History*, vols I–XII. Oxford: Oxford University Press.

Tutu, Desmond. 2007/2008. "We Do Not Need Climate Change Apartheid in Adaptation." *Human Development Report*. New York: United Nations.

Tversky, Amos, and Daniel Kahneman. 1974. "Judgment under Uncertainty: Heuristics and Biases." *Science 185*: 1124–31.

United Nations. 1983. *Process of Preparation of the Environmental Perspective to the Year 2000 and Beyond*. Retrieved June 10, 2010 (http://www.un.org/documents/ga/res/381a38r161.htm).

United States Bureau of the Census. 2010. "World Population Growth." Retrieved September 16, 2010 (http://www.census.gov/ipc/www/idb/worldpopgraph.php).

United States Chamber of Commerce. 2009. "Climate Change." Retrieved October 25, 2010 (http://www.uschamber.com/issues/environment/five-positions-energy-and-environment).

United States Department of Energy. 2008. *20 Percent Wind Energy by 2030.* Retrieved October 26, 2010 (http://www.doe.gov/windenergy).

United States Department of Energy and Environmental Protection Agency. 2010. "How Can a Gallon of Gasoline Produce 20 pounds of Carbon Dioxide?" Retrieved September 16, 2010 (http://www.fueleconomy.gov/Feg/co2.shtml).

United States Energy Information Administration. 2010. *Gasoline Explained.* Retrieved July 19, 2010 (http: //www.eia.gov/energyexplained).

United States Geological Survey. 2010. *Alaskan National Wildlife Refuge: Amount of Oil.* Retrieved July 6, 2010 (http://www.usgs.gov).

University of California, San Diego. 2010. "Keeling Curve." Retrieved July 1, 2010 (http://earthguide.ucsd.edu/globalchange/keeling_curve/01.html).

Urry, John. 2010. "Consuming the Planet to Excess." *Theory, Culture and Society 27*: 191–212.

Wald, Matthew L. 2009. "Can Nuclear Power Compete?" *Scientific American Earth 3.0* (Special Issue. March 17): 26–33.

Washington, Richard, Christel Bouet, Guy Cautenet, Elizabeth Mackenzie, Ian Ashpole, Sebastian Englestaedter, Gil Lizcano, Gideon M. Henderson, Kerstin Schepanski, and Ina Tegen. 2009. "Dust as a Tipping Element: The Bodélé Depression, Chad." *Publications of the National Academy of Sciences 106*(49): 64–71.

Watkins, Kevin. 2006. *Beyond Scarcity: Power, Poverty and the Global Water Crisis.* United Nations: Human Development Report 2006. Hampshire, UK and New York: Palgrave Macmillan.

Watkins, Kevin. 2007/2008. *Human Development Report for 2007/2008: Fighting Climate Change: Human Solidarity in a Divided World*, United Nations: Human Development Programme. Hampshire, UK and New York: Palgrave Macmillan. Retrieved October 26, 2010 (http://hdr.undp.org/en/media/HDR_20072008_EN_Complete.pdf).

Webb, Richard. 2009. "Tax Carbon and Give the Money to the People." *New Scientist* (September 12): 36.

Weisbach, David, Gernot Wagner, Janet E. Milne, Kenneth R. Richards, and Nathaniel Keohane. 2008. "Carbon Tax vs. Cap-and-Trade." *Bulletin of the Atomic Scientists* (July 6). Accessed online at http://thebulletin.org/.../carbon-tax-vs-cap-and-trade.

Wooten, J. Timothy, Catherine A. Pfister, and James D. Forester. 2008. "Dynamic Patterns and Ecological Impacts of Declining Ocean pH in a High-Resolution Multi-Year Data Set." *Proceedings of the National Academy of Sciences* 105: 18848–53.

World Bank. 2010. "World Development Indicators, 2010." Retrieved October 25, 2010 (data.worldbank.org).

Yu, Jiang. 2007. Cited by Thomas L. Friedman in "The Power of Green." *New York Times Magazine* (April 15).

Glossary/Index

Note: Page numbers followed by "n" refer to notes.

350 Movement: founded by Bill McKibben and his colleagues in preparation for the Copenhagen talks on climate change in 2009. The organization's goal was to set a target, 350 ppm of CO_2 in the atmosphere, to focus the talks and galvanize action on climate change. It is now a global movement focused on reducing CO_2 in the atmosphere. It identifies actions that local communities, colleges, and individuals can take to achieve the goal of 350 ppm. 56

A

adaptation: in the case of climate science it refers to those actions we can take to reduce the impacts of climate change such as building sea walls, developing drought-resistant crops, and developing and using non-fossil-based fuels 58, 67

aerosols: refers to precipitates that make up part of our atmosphere which, depending on their properties, can either lead to a build-up of heat or have a cooling effect. Sulfate aerosols, caused by burning coal and volcanic eruptions, have a cooling effect because they bounce solar radiation back into space. Black carbon or soot is another aerosol that can cause cooling or heating, depending on whether it is deposited on the ground (leading to melting of glaciers) or is in the atmosphere (leading to cooling). 6, 63

Africa 1, 15, 16, 41, 63

agricultural yields 61

Alaskan National Wildlife Refuge (ANWR) 43

albedo effect: refers to the reflective properties of those things (glaciers, snow, white roof tops) that reflect solar radiation back into space and therefore reduce the build-up of heat in the Earth's atmosphere 6, 7

Allen, Myles 22, 60

alternative lifestyles movements 51, 52–53

Amazonian rainforest 7, 8

American Policy Center 28

American Psychological Association 44

anchor: our cognitive bias in terms of what we already know, which means we do not look for new or disconfirming information 42

Anderegg, William, et al. 26

Antarctic 9

Anthropocene: a term used by some to describe a new geological era caused by human beings. It has no specific date but is seen as beginning with the rise of the Industrial Revolution. The term is made up of two roots: anthropo (human) and cene (new geological age). 3

anticipated risk: those risks where we know the likelihood that something will actually happen 35

Arctic 2, 9, 14, 49, 63

argon 5

Assembly Bill 32 30–31

atmosphere, Earth's 4–6

Ausubel, Jesse 61

Avatar 38

B

Barringer, Felicity 21

behavior, human 53, 66–67

biofuels 65

biomass: is the total mass of living matter—animal and plant—in a given environment. It is organic matter from which energy can be derived. 65

biosphere 3

Blair, Tony 55

Bodele Depression: a desert area in sub-Saharan Africa (Chad) across which high winds blow carrying sedimentary material as far away as the Amazon, providing nutrients for the rainforest 7

bottled water 16–17

Boykoff, Maxwell and Jules 21

Brennan, Philip V. 36

British Antarctic Survey 25–26

Brown, Lester 17, 50

Brundtland Commission 13

Bush, George W. 22, 23

C

California

 Assembly Bill 32 30–31

 happiness in 43

China

    buying up land in Africa 17

    carbon emissions 15, 56, 57

    energy demands of 51n

    energy sources 60

    meat consumption 66

    wind turbines 64

climate change: refers to the fact that concentrations of CO_2 in the atmosphere are increasing, which will lead to global warming in some areas and cooling in others. It also refers to the consequences of the build-up of CO_2, which could include rising sea levels, droughts, violent storms, species extinction, and the collapse of entire ecosystems. 7, 24–27

    and assessing risk 42–47

    deniers of 10–11, 24–30, 36–37

    environmental skepticism 36

    environmental skepticism and 28, 29, 32

    evidence of 1–2

    global inequalities in effects of 15–16

    moral framing of 36, 39–40

    organizations campaigning against 28–30, 31

    partisan splits on 30–31

    reasons for failure to act on 66–67

    religion and 40

    scientific consensus 9–11, 26

    shaping of public opinion on 20–24, 28, 30, 31

    tipping points for 6–9

    understanding size of problem 41–42

    world views of 37–39

    see also solutions to climate change

Climategate 32–33

Club of Rome 11

coal 29, 31, 60, 64

Collapse: How Societies Choose to Fail or Succeed (Toynbee) 12

confirmation bias: our tendency to seek information that supports our positions 42

consensus, scientific 9–11, 26

conservative think tanks (CTTs) 28

constant gases: stable gases that make up the bulk of our dry atmosphere including nitrogen (78 percent), oxygen (21 percent), and argon (1 percent). These are not included in the calculation of greenhouse gas emissions. 5

    see **greenhouse gases** for the variable gases.

consumption 16, 17, 53
    of meat 66
    overconsumption 59
Cooney, Phillip 23
Copenhagen Accord 57
Copenhagen Climate Summit 2009 33, 50, 54, 56–57, 62
creationism 40
Crichton, Michael 21, 22

D
Darwin, Charles 40
The Day After Tomorrow 20–21
deforestation 63
Democrats 30–31
developing nations
    actions needed on climate change in 63–64
    carbon emission targets 33, 54, 57
    children in 57
    energy needs 51n
    transfer of technologies to 33, 57, 64
Di-Aping, Lumumba 57
Diamond, Jared 12
Dickens, Charles 51
discount rate: a term used by economists that embeds two concepts: the anticipated
    rate of return on capital over an extended period of time and the economic welfare
    of different households over the same period of time. Given the rate of inflation,
    for example, $1 million today might only be worth $200,000 in ten years. Or, in
    ten years people will be wealthier than we are today, so they should bear the bur-
    den of investing to reduce carbon dioxide in the atmosphere. 55–56
Dubai 51
Dunning–Kruger effect: the idea that people who do not know much, do not know
    they do not know much, and therefore seek no additional information 42

E
Earth 2, 3–4
Economist 50, 56, 57, 63
ecosystem: a system formed by the interaction of a community of organisms and
    their physical environment. Ecosystems vary in size but include humans, plants,
    animals, soil, and water and refer to the complex relationships between them. A
    healthy ecosystem is one in balance and is sustainable. 1

emails at University of East Anglia 32–33

energy 51n, 64–65

    costs of 60–61

    renewable 30, 61, 62, 64, 65

Engels, Frederick 51

environmental amnesia: our lack of understanding of what is happening in our own biosphere and lack of recognition of the degradation of the environment 44

Environmental Protection Agency (EPA) 23, 31

environmental skepticism 28, 29, 32, 36

Erlich, Paul and Anne 59

An Essay on the Principle of Population (Malthus) 11

Europe 1–2, 6, 11, 15, 67

external costs: in the case of the environment it refers to the fact that the price we pay for a good does not reflect its true costs, such as pollution of the air or water. The price of a gallon of gasoline, for example, does not reflect the true costs of the gas, which would include costs of pollution, urban sprawl, protection of a national supply of oil, etc. 48

ExxonMobil 28, 29

F

failed state: a state which fails to provide basic necessities for its citizens (food, water, and shelter), adequate medical care (as measured by infant mortality and life expectancy), and is not recognized by its citizens as legitimate. An index has been developed by *Foreign Policy* which compares states on 12 measures. 17

fisheries 8, 12

Flannery, Tim 3, 4

fossil fuels 6, 18, 53, 60, 65

Friedman, Thomas 62

future generations, concern for 54–56

G

Gaia hypothesis: a theory of James Lovelock that the living and non-living parts of the Earth form a complex interactive system that may be thought of as a single organism 3

gasoline

    burning 41, 48

    real price of 48, 52, 54, 66–67

    statistics on consumption of 65

Gelbspan, Ross 21, 29

geoengineering 65–66

global warming 4–6
    arguments denying humans as cause of 10–11
    as a cause of worry 46
    evidence of 1–2
    inequalities of 15–16
    media coverage 21
    policy of George W. Bush on 23
    psychology of public thinking on 44
    reasons for lack of understanding about 27
The Global Warming Swindle 24–25
Goodstein, Eban 39
Gore, Al 22–23, 24, 28, 32, 36
greenhouse gases (GHGs): those gases that make up Earth's atmosphere and trap heat. The main greenhouse gases are water vapor, carbon dioxide, methane, nitrous oxide, ozone and chlorofluorocarbons (CFCs). The chief driver of climate change is the build-up of CO_2 in the atmosphere and comes from transportation, energy production, and industry. 4, 58, 63
    Assembly Bill 32 30–31
    debate at Copenhagen on cutting 54, 56–57
    declared as pollutants in U.S. 31
    Kyoto Protocol 1997 22
Gulf oil spill 2010 18, 46–47, 55

H
Hansen, James 57
Hardin, Garrett 49
The Hartwell Paper 62
Hawken, Paul 61
Heartland Institute 28–29, 30
Heritage Foundation 28
Hoffert, Marty 62
Holdren, John 38
Holocene era: a geological era beginning from 10–12,000 years ago with the rise of human civilization. It has been a period of stable climate. 2
    see **Anthropocene**.
Hopkins, Rob 53
Houghton, John 25, 26
Hubbert, M. King 13
Hubbert peak theory: refers to the ideas of M. King Hubbert, who predicted that oil production would peak at some point, which would never be surpassed, and then

would decline over time (as would all other natural resources). His ideas recognize that all natural systems have finite limits and that the costs of natural resources will increase. Many experts believe we reached peak oil production in 2010, later than Hubbert had predicted it would occur. 13–14

Hulme, Mike 37, 38

human rights 37

Hurricane Katrina 11, 44, 55

I

Ice Age 8, 9

ice, melting 2, 7, 9, 14, 49, 63

An Inconvenient Truth 22–23, 36

India 2, 6, 7, 16

Industrial Revolution 1, 4, 51

inequalities, global 15–16, 37, 63, 67

Information Council on the Environment (ICE) 29

insurance companies 55

Intergovernmental Panel on Climate Change (IPCC) models 9, 23, 25, 32, 33, 38, 66

International Energy Agency 57

J

Jackson, Lisa 31

Jacques, Peter 27

James, William 45

Jefferson, Thomas 51

Jensen, Derrick 52

Jiang Yu 57

Jones, Phil 32

K

Kahneman, Daniel 42, 43

Keeling, Charles David 4–5

Keeling Curve: named after Charles David Keeling, it refers to a graph developed by Keeling to measure the concentration of CO_2 in the atmosphere beginning in 1958 at the Mauna Loa Observatory in Hawaii. The graph shows a continued upward curve with variations during the spring and fall due to photosynthesis. 5

King, David 33, 63

Klein, Naomi 46

Krauthammer, Charles 57
Krugman, Paul 54, 60
Kyoto Protocol 1997 22, 33

L
Ladurie, Emmanuel le Roy 25
laws of thermodynamics: the first two laws are that matter can neither be created nor destroyed and that all systems tend to entropy (or run down). The laws are important to the study of Earth's systems and an understanding that all systems have finite limits and that once natural resources are used up they are gone forever. 27, 40
Leiserowitz, Anthony 21
The Limits to Growth (Meadows) 11
Limits to Growth: The 30-Year Update 12
Little Ice Age 24–25
local economies 52, 53, 63
Longfellow, Brenda 37
Lovelock, James 3
Lovins, Hunter and Amory 61
Lowry, Rich 32

M
Malthus, Thomas 11
Mandia, Scott 24–25
Mars 3, 4
Marx, Karl 51
McKibben, Bill 52
Meadows, Donella 11
meat consumption 66
media reporting on global warming 21
Meredith, John 28
methane: a greenhouse gas that has 25 times more potential to trap heat than CO_2. Like CO_2 it changes the amount of solar energy entering and leaving the Earth's atmosphere. 3, 5, 6, 7, 31
see **greenhouse gases** and **radiative forcing**
Milankovitch cycles: refer to the fact that the Earth goes through three natural cycles of heating and cooling based on *eccentricity* (shape of the Earth's orbit around the Sun every 100,000 years); *precession*, or the wobbling of the Earth on its axis every 21–23,000 years; and *tilt* relative to the plane of the Earth, which occurs every 41,000 years. 10

mitigation: in the case of climate science it refers to those actions we can take to reduce the build-up of carbon dioxide in the air, such as reducing our consumption of fossil fuels, or sequestering the carbon emitted from coal-burning plants. Mitigation efforts focus primarily on increasing efficiencies, reducing consumption, and driving less or using cars with greater fuel efficiency. 58, 67

monsoons: seasonal variation in rainfall caused by the asymmetric heating of the land and the sea, which in turn causes shifts in wind patterns followed by changes in precipitation. It often refers to the heavy summer rains in India, caused by winds blowing off the Indian Ocean. 7

moral framing: framing discussions about such things as climate change and its consequences in terms of right or wrong 36, 39–40

ocean conveyor belt: refers to the circulation of water from warmer to colder regions in the world's oceans. The circulation begins in the far Pacific and ends in the North Atlantic, taking 1,000 years to complete. Some have argued that this conveyor belt could be slowed or stopped by the rapid melting of glaciers in the Arctic 8–9

see also **thermohaline circulation**

R

radiative forcing: refers to changes in the amount of solar radiation entering and leaving Earth's atmosphere. Carbon dioxide causes a reduction in the amount of solar radiation leaving the atmosphere, which increases temperatures. 6

rainforest, Amazonian 7, 8

Rayner, Steve 49, 50

relative thinking: as the term implies we compare events, e.g., we compare immediate versus long-term benefits and choose the immediate benefit. We compare gains and losses, and because we fear loss more than we value gain, we act to preserve the status quo. 43

religion 27, 37, 40, 58

renewable energies 61, 62, 64, 65
in California 30

Republicans 30–31, 42

Revelle, Roger 5

Rifkin, Jeremy 51n

risk assessment 42–47
see also **anticipated risk; perceived risk**

Rockford 44–45

Russia 14, 59, 61

S

Saudi Arabia 17, 33, 61

Saunders, Sam C. 35

Schkade, David A. 43

science, lack of public understanding of 26–27

scientific consensus 9–11, 26

Schwarzenegger, Arnold 30

sea levels 2, 7, 30, 41

Shuman, Michael 52

Socolow, Robert 61

solar energy 64

solutions to climate change
changing our behavior 53, 66–67
and concern for future generations 54–56
deciding who should pay 56–58
geoengineering 65–66
and movements in opposition to way we live now 52–53
new technologies 64–65
optimistic views on 61–62
payment methods to reduce carbon emissions 53–54

pessimistic views on 62

solving the problems 50–52, 58–61

strategies for action 62–64

type of problem to be solved 49–50

soot

see **aerosols**

Soron, Dennis 37

stabilization wedge: a strategy that can help to reduce carbon emissions 62

State of Fear 21–22

Steingraber, Sandra 44

Stern, Nicholas 55–56

Stern Review 55–56

The Study of History (Toynbee) 12

sunspots and solar flares: these are of interest to climate scientists because sunspots occur on an 11-year cycle and cause a variation in the amount of solar radiation coming from the Sun. Solar radiation has been relatively constant over the course of the last 2,000 years and is not an explanation for recent changes in Earth's climate. When sunspots are most intense they release bursts of radiation (solar flares) which, if strong enough, can disrupt telecommunications on Earth. 10, 24

sustainability: a term used by the Brundtland Commission of the United Nations that defines sustainability as development that meets the needs of present generations without compromising the ability of future generations to meet their needs (biological, social, economic) 13, 49, 57, 66

Sweeney, James 31

Swim, Janet 43, 44

systems theory: an interdisciplinary approach that considers any system greater than the sum of its parts. Earth is seen as a single system composed of many interrelated parts (oceans, forests, atmosphere, soil, etc.) with a change in any part causing a change in the entire system. It is the basis of climate science. 3, 11

T

Tainter, Joseph 12

technology 19, 60, 61, 62, 67

transfer of 33, 57, 64

theory of moral hazards: suggests our behavior will be constrained only if we know what the costs (moral and/or economic) of our action will be, or if we suffer the consequences of our action 53

thermohaline circulation: refers to the circulation of the ocean currents caused by heat (therm) and salinity (haline). 8

see **ocean conveyor belt**

tipping points: a term used by some scientists to describe the point at which the Earth's systems tip out of balance, leading to catastrophic changes such as droughts, rising sea levels, dramatic changes in temperature, and the collapse of the biological systems that support human life as we have known it for the last 10,000 years. 6–9

see **systems theory**

University Readers™
Reading Materials Evolved.

Introducing the

SOCIAL ISSUES COLLECTION

A Routledge/University Readers Custom Library for Teaching

Customizing course material for innovative and excellent teaching in sociology has never been easier or more effective!

Choose from a collection of more than 300 readings from Routledge, Taylor & Francis, and other publishers to make a custom anthology that suits the needs of your social problems/ social inequality, and social issues courses.

All readings have been aptly chosen by academic editors and our authors and organized by topic and author.

Online tool makes it easy for busy instructors:

1. Simply select your favorite Routledge and Taylor & Francis readings, and add any other required course material, including your own.

2. Choose the order of the readings, pick a binding, and customize a cover.

3. One click will post your materials for students to buy. They can purchase print or digital packs, and we ship direct to their door within two weeks of ordering!

More information at www.socialissuescollection.com

Contact information: Call your Routledge sales rep, or
Becky Smith at University Readers, 800-200-3908 ext. 18, bsmith@universityreaders.com
Steve Rutter at Routledge, 207-434-2102, Steve.Rutter@taylorandfrancis.com.

Routledge
Taylor & Francis Group
an **informa** business